Rhyming Tots

Edited By Jenni Bannister

First published in Great Britain in 2016 by:

Coltsfoot Drive
Peterborough
PE2 9BF
Telephone: 01733 890066
Website: www.youngwriters.co.uk

All Rights Reserved
Book Design by Ben Reeves
© Copyright Contributors 2016
SB ISBN 978-1-78624-374-4
Printed and bound in the UK by BookPrintingUK
Website: www.bookprintinguk.com
YB0278N

Foreword

Young Writers was established in 1991 with the aim of encouraging writing skills in young people and giving them the opportunity to see their work in print. Poetry is a wonderful way to introduce young children to the idea of rhyme and rhythm and helps learning and development of communication, language and literacy skills.

'My First Poem' was created to introduce nursery and preschool children to this wonderful world of poetry. They were given a template to fill in with their own words, creating a poem that was all about them.

We are proud to present the resulting collection of personal and touching poems in this anthology, which can be treasured for years to come.

Jenni Bannister
Editorial Manager

Contents

ABC Kidz Nursery, Edgware

Bivas Sapkota (4)	1
Minhah Zakir (4)	2
Musa Jukaku (4)	3

Ashgrove Farm Day Nursery, Chester

Thomas Christopher Drewe (4)	4

Chedworth Preschool, Cheltenham

Tristan Hatherell (4)	5
Thomas Fletcher (3)	6
Logan Pitts (4)	7
Agatha McMahon (4)	8
Eva Huckson-Winter (3)	9
Beatrice Hayman-Joyce (3)	10
Emilia Plekaniec (3)	11
Leo Morgan (3)	12
Toby Kittirungwathana (4)	13
Evie Brock (3)	14

Chieveley Preschool, Newbury

Rufus Brown (3)	15
Esmae Mountain (3)	16

Comberton Day Nursery, London

Amrit Kaur (3)	17
Jorel Attoh Quarshie (3)	18

Esme Young (3) ... continued

Esme Young (3)	19
Bobby Parker Randall (4)	20
Levie Sandoz (4)	21
E'loheka Oppong-Frimpong (3)	22
Alexander Nakos (3)	23
Oluwatosin Niyi-Olowu (3)	24

Eaton Mill Nursery, Milton Keynes

Colbie Marie Flower (4)	25
Lena Cooper (4)	26
Warith Mpalanzi (4)	27
Dasia Milagros La Barbera (4)	28
Reuben Thomas Peter Lowe (4)	29
Inioluwa Badru (3)	30
Esther Aremu (4)	31
Sadia Tasnim (4)	32
Keira Evelyn Simpson (4)	33
Abubakar Amin Yusuf (4)	34
Tolbert Kofi Agyeman (4)	35
Ella Stodart (3)	36
Zunairah Hasan (4)	37
Tayah Puchner (2)	38
Joe McNab (4)	39
Ellis louis john Quailey (4)	40
Leo Segebrecht (3)	41
Fabian Watts (3)	42
Ashleigh Turney-Harris (4)	43
Ollie Ledster (4)	44
Elsie-Mae Daniella Barnett (3)	45
Poppy-Mae Mintram (3)	46
Kira Morris (4)	47

Tillie James (4)	48
Freddie Keep (4)	49
Richard Abioye (3)	50
Lotti Perry (2)	51
David Bruno Carneiro Ferreira (3)	52
Mia Hurst (4)	53
Francis Ellen Ridge (3)	54
Leo Charles Marlow (4)	55
Skye Gillian Johnson (3)	56
Mylah Biscoe (3)	57
Samuel Brindle (2)	58
Callum Michael Mendes O'Brien (4)	59
Jasper Beddall (4)	60
Henry Williams (3)	61
Zayyan Anwar Miah (3)	62
Yunus Hussain (3)	63
Nico Rutter (5)	64
Charlotte Butler (3)	65
Bonnie Jae Hurst (3)	66
Sophie Faulkner (4)	67
Fearne Cowie (3)	68

Fellowship House Children's Centre, London

Daniel Andrei Cosovat (4)	69

Happy Valley Preschool, Newhaven

Olivia Warren (2)	70
Isabella Deacon (3)	71
Connor Pryor (4)	72
Sophie Walker (2)	73
Mia Deacon (3)	74
Charlie Bassett (3)	75
Tommy Bentley (4)	76
Ashleigh Streatfield-Mollon (4)	77
Becky Hector (3)	78

Lexi Cranmer (4)	79
Luka Lambert (4)	80
Max Huggett (4)	81
Mya Ridgway (3)	82
Lexi-Elisse Bowles (4)	83
Paige-Summer Greaney (3)	84
Lilly-Mae Dewdney (4)	85
Jamie-Sienna Greaney (2)	86
Ocean Ridgway (4)	87
Emre Endogan (3)	88
Alexander Bentley (2)	89
Aleah-Louise Bowles-Taplin (4)	90

Little Friends Preschool, Banbridge

Jackson McKee (4)	91
Anna Parkes (4)	92
Jayden Campbell (3)	93
Juliana Rachel Nelson (4)	94
Lucy Black (4)	95
Alexandra Davidson (4)	96
Alfie Moore (4)	97
Ethan Young (4)	98
Brogan Malone (4)	99
Masen Paul McKiverigan-Thompson (3)	100
Katie McKnight (3)	101
Matthew King (4)	102
Isaac William Mathers (4)	103

Little House Day Nursery & Preschool, London

Benjamin Rafferty	104
Samora Banda (3)	105
Rayea Anastasia Scott (2)	106
Henry Scully	107
Olivia Rayfield (3)	108
Victor Bacher	109
Filippo Thomas Monetto (3)	110

Livia	111

Little Rascals Nurseries, Tunbridge Wells

James Jaswal (4)	112
Ava Cannacott (3)	113
Isla Bysouth (4)	114
Claire Hubbard (3)	115
Leo Heathcoat (4)	116
Noah Swaffield-Robinson (4)	117
Henry James Shepherd (4)	118
Evie Simpson (3)	119
Jack Levett (4)	120
Marcy Winter (3)	121
Holden Nouyou (4)	122
Finlay Evans (4)	123
Joshua Wheeler (4)	124
Sophie Loftus (4)	125

Pinewood Family Group Preschool, Farnborough

Jaxon Duddy (4)	126
Simbarashe Kayden Mapeta (4)	127
Oscar Mason Eales (4)	128
Alfee-Jai Sterriker-Dixon (2)	129
Rebecca Emily Stock (2)	130
Emily Abbots (3)	131
Summer Facchini (2)	132
Bruno Alexander Ford (3)	133
Sashwat Kiran Gurung (3)	134
Hazel Violet Booth (4)	135
Amelia Cooles (3)	136
Astley Povey (3)	137
Riley Willis (3)	138

Play Time Under 5s, Hove

Betty Rose Grice (4)	139

Puddleducks Day Nursery, Baldock

Isabelle Levett (4)	140
Nina White (3)	141
Alex Picard-Cook (3)	142
Oscar Lynam (4)	143
Aubrey Murphy-Wearmouth (3)	144
Cerys Evans (3)	145
Oskar Francis (4)	146
Amelia Ramirez-Baez (4)	147
Frankie Zwirner (3)	148
Sofia Jones (4)	149
Maxwell Vinyard (3)	150
Iona Thompson-Nisbet (4)	151
Edward Rofe (3)	152
Samuel Evans (3)	153
Keira Parkinson (3)	154
Zoe Wood (4)	155
Aoife Doherty (3)	156
Jessica Green (3)	157
Bethany Hemmings (3)	158
Noah Fitzgerald (3)	159
Benjamin Cape (3)	160
Mason Hunt (3)	161
Stefan Centala (3)	162
Luca Casalini (3)	163
Erin Holly Robinson (3)	164
Summer Haer (3)	165
Zavier Lemaitre (4)	166
Cadi Hâf Bradford (3)	167
Isabel Gale (4)	168
Matthew Pike (3)	169
Jacob Adam King (4)	170
Zoe Barr (4)	171
William Ioan Davies (3)	172
Brandon Delaney (3)	173
Max Middleton (3)	174

Red Fox Day Nursery, Marlow

Finlay Leach (3)	175
Harry Shillito (3)	176
Jess Rooney (3)	177

St Gabriel's Playgroup, Billingshurst

Cooper Burstow (3)	178
George Evans (4)	179
Isabelle Carter (3)	180
Maddie Twaddle (4)	181
Chloe Tillotson (4)	182
Raphael White (3)	183
Jayden James Foster-Hopkins (4)	184
Brooke Hyde (4)	185

St John's Playgroup, Harrogate

Rosie Faith Bryan (4)	186
Freya Manley (4)	187
Charlie Wilson	188
Dillan Foster (3)	189
Daniel Hewson (4)	190
Hazel Alison Thurley (3)	191
Lucy Nicholls (4)	192
Kayleigh Louise Carney (4)	193

Starfish Day Nursery, Fareham

Nathan Rickman (4)	194
Isabelle Rose Cox (3)	195
Caleb Allen (3)	196

Starlings Preschool, Basingstoke

Chloé Dos Santos (3)	197
Owen Stephen Leaney (3)	198

Logan Billington (4)	199
Emilia Wilkinson (2)	200
Marcus Goddard (2)	201
Isla Grace Amos (3)	202
Evie Vickery (3)	203
Kaci Thomas-Graham (3)	204
Evie-Mae Field (3)	205
Michael Waring (4)	206
Callum Riley Embleton (4)	207
Harrison Lee Brian Ford (3)	208
Medeea Ana-Maria Biro (3)	209
Frankie Gordon Potter (3)	210
Olivia Rogers (4)	211
Tytus Mrozowski (4)	212
Keilan Farmer (3)	213
Ella Robertson (3)	214
Jalika Lehannah Camara (3)	215
Al-Mahdi Uddin (4)	216
Siddhartha Gurung (3)	217
Toby Cowie (3)	218
Nathan Jones (3)	219
Zac Roberts (3)	220
Ethan Smith (4)	221
Jimmy Say (2)	222

Therfield Village Preschool, Royston

Max Barrett (4)	223
Charley Challis (3)	224
Thomas Joseph Benson (3)	225

Tiddlywinks Preschool, Colchester

Ezri Marsh (3)	226
Amelia Rose Kemp (3)	227
Micky Bowman (2)	228
Max Alfie Woodhurst	229
Penny Duckworth (3)	230
James Kettle (2)	231

Leo George Woodhurst	232
Sienna Violet Payne (2)	233
George Edward Snowling (4)	234

Wayside, Croydon

Lewis Eric Benstead (4)	235

Woodend Nursery, Aberdeen

Logan Angus (4)	236
Ellie Kate Gray (4)	237
Chloe MacKenzie (4)	238
Joe McGunnigle (4)	239
Ademayowa Adeshina (4)	240
Brendan Mitchell (4)	241
Toby Benjamin Cook (4)	242
Emily Charlotte Pope (4)	243

The Poems

My First Poem

My name is **Bivas** and I go to preschool,
My best friend is **Minhah**, who is really cool.
I watch **Pop** on TV,
Playing **block 3D** is lots of fun for me.
I just love **pasta** to eat,
And sometimes **Coke** for a treat.
Red is a colour I like a lot,
My **Spider-Man** is the best present I ever got.
My favourite people are **my family**, who are gems,
So this, my first poem, is just for them!

Bivas Sapkota (4)
ABC Kidz Nursery, Edgware

My First Poem

My name is Minhah and I go to preschool,
My best friend is Bivas, who is really cool.
I watch Come Outside on TV,
Playing games is lots of fun for me.
I just love potatoes to eat,
And sometimes bubblegum for a treat.
Blue is a colour I like a lot,
My dolls are the best present I ever got.
My favourite person is Mummy, who is a gem,
So this, my first poem, is just for them!

Minhah Zakir (4)
ABC Kidz Nursery, Edgware

My First Poem

My name is **Musa** and I go to preschool,
My best friend is **Abdullah**, who is really cool.
I watch **games** on TV,
Playing **Lego** is lots of fun for me.
I just love **noodles** to eat,
And sometimes **a lolly** for a treat.
Orange is a colour I like a lot,
My **mum and dad** are the best present I ever got.
My favourite person is **Nuh**, who is a gem,
So this, my first poem, is just for them!

Musa Jukaku (4)
ABC Kidz Nursery, Edgware

My First Poem

My name is Thomas and I go to preschool,
My best friends are Ollie and Elliott, who are really cool.
I watch The Incredibles on TV,
Playing battles is lots of fun for me.
I just love lamb to eat,
And sometimes sweeties for a treat.
Blue is a colour I like a lot,
My castle is the best present I ever got.
My favourite people are Mummy and Daddy, who are gems,
So this, my first poem, is just for them!

Thomas Christopher Drewe (4)
Ashgrove Farm Day Nursery, Chester

My First Poem

My name is **Tristan** and I go to preschool,
My best friend is **Toby**, who is really cool.
I watch **cars** on TV,
Playing **Lego** is lots of fun for me.
I just love **pancakes and pasta** to eat,
And sometimes **cake** for a treat.
Red, yellow, green and orange are colours I like a lot,
My **toy truck** is the best present I ever got.
My favourite people are **Mummy and Daddy**, who are gems,
So this, my first poem, is just for them!

Tristan Hatherell (4)

Chedworth Preschool, Cheltenham

My First Poem

My name is **Thomas** and I go to preschool,
My best friend is **Tristan**, who is really cool.
I watch **PAW Patrol** on TV,
Playing **buses** is lots of fun for me.
I just love **Slurpy Eddy** to eat,
And sometimes **strawberries** for a treat.
Yellow is a colour I like a lot,
My **tractor** is the best present I ever got.
My favourite person is **Mummy**, who is a gem,
So this, my first poem, is just for them!

Thomas Fletcher (3)
Chedworth Preschool, Cheltenham

My First Poem

My name is Logan and I go to preschool,
My best friend is Eva, who is really cool.
I watch Buzz Lightyear on TV,
Playing babies is lots of fun for me.
I just love apples and bananas to eat,
And sometimes cupcakes for a treat.
Blue is a colour I like a lot,
My dinosaur and car are the best presents I ever got.
My favourite person is Troy, who is a gem,
So this, my first poem, is just for them!

Logan Pitts (4)
Chedworth Preschool, Cheltenham

My First Poem

My name is Agatha and I go to preschool,
My best friends are Eleanor, Evie and Beatrice,
who are really cool.
I watch Peppa Pig on TV,
Playing with everything is lots of fun for me.
I just love sausage rolls to eat,
And sometimes chocolate for a treat.
Blue is a colour I like a lot,
My teddy is the best present I ever got.
My favourite people are Orla and Briony, who are gems,
So this, my first poem, is just for them!

Agatha McMahon (4)
Chedworth Preschool, Cheltenham

My First Poem

My name is **Eva** and I go to preschool,
My best friend is **Logie**, who is really cool.
I watch **Mickey Mouse** on TV,
Playing **cars** is lots of fun for me.
I just love **chicken** to eat,
And sometimes **sweeties** for a treat.
Pink, like my pink sparkly top is a colour I like a lot,
My **blue and pink Barbies** are the best present I ever got.
My favourite people are **Mummy and Daddy**, who are gems,
So this, my first poem, is just for them!

Eva Huckson-Winter (3)
Chedworth Preschool, Cheltenham

My First Poem

My name is Beatrice and I go to preschool,
My best friend is Agatha, who is really cool.
I watch Peter Rabbit on TV,
Playing puzzles is lots of fun for me.
I just love chips to eat,
And sometimes chocolate eggs for a treat.
Pink is a colour I like a lot,
My baby and bath are the best presents I ever got.
My favourite person is Mummy, who is a gem,
So this, my first poem, is just for them!

Beatrice Hayman-Joyce (3)
Chedworth Preschool, Cheltenham

My First Poem

My name is Emilia and I go to preschool,
My best friend is Mummy, who is really cool.
I watch Peppa Pig on TV,
Playing Play-Doh is lots of fun for me.
I just love sausage to eat,
And sometimes ice cream for a treat.
Green is a colour I like a lot,
My toys are the best present I ever got.
My favourite people are Mummy and Daddy,
who are gems,
So this, my first poem, is just for them!

Emilia Plekaniec (3)
Chedworth Preschool, Cheltenham

My First Poem

My name is Leo and I go to preschool,
My best friends are Daddy and Mummy, who are really cool.
I watch racing cars on TV,
Playing cars is lots of fun for me.
I just love apples to eat,
And sometimes chocolate for a treat.
Blue is a colour I like a lot,
My helicopter is the best present I ever got.
My favourite person is Mummy, who is a gem,
So this, my first poem, is just for them.

Leo Morgan (3)
Chedworth Preschool, Cheltenham

My First Poem

My name is **Toby** and I go to preschool,
My best friend is **Tristan**, who is really cool.
I watch **Spider-Man** on TV,
Playing **cooking** is lots of fun for me.
I just love **pizza** to eat,
And sometimes **chocolate** for a treat.
Green is a colour I like a lot,
My **castle** is the best present I ever got.
My favourite person is **my brother, Charlie**,
who is a gem,
So this, my first poem, is just for them!

Toby Kittirungwathana (4)
Chedworth Preschool, Cheltenham

My First Poem

My name is Evie and I go to preschool,
My best friends are Agatha, Beatrice and Eleanor, who are really cool.
I watch Peppa Pig on TV,
Playing doctors is lots of fun for me.
I just love cheese and pasta to eat,
And sometimes choccy buttons for a treat.
Dark Pink is a colour I like a lot,
My Barbie dolls are the best present I ever got.
My favourite person is Rosie Posy, my sister, who is a gem,
So this, my first poem, is just for them!

Evie Brock (3)

Chedworth Preschool, Cheltenham

My First Poem

My name is Rufus and I go to preschool,
My best friend is Fern, who is really cool.
I watch PAW Patrol on TV,
Playing cars is lots of fun for me.
I just love pancakes to eat,
And sometimes oranges for a treat.
Purple, orange and yellow are colours I like a lot,
My train and fire engine are the best presents I ever got.
My favourite person is Eva, who is a gem,
So this, my first poem, is just for them!

Rufus Brown (3)
Chieveley Preschool, Newbury

My First Poem

My name is Esmae and I go to preschool,
My best friend is Holly, who is really cool.
I watch PAW Patrol on TV,
Playing cars is lots of fun for me.
I just love macaroni cheese to eat,
And sometimes chocolate milkshake for a treat.
Red is a colour I like a lot,
My Barnacles, Kwazii and Peso are the best presents I ever got.
My favourite person is Varinia, who is a gem,
So this, my first poem, is just for them!

Esmae Mountain (3)
Chieveley Preschool, Newbury

My First Poem

My name is **Amrit** and I go to preschool,
My best friend is **Anita**, who is really cool.
I watch **Peppa Pig and Masha and the Bear** on TV,
Playing **with fruits and toys** is lots of fun for me.
I just love **red and green grapes** to eat,
And sometimes a **Milky Bar** for a treat.
Red and purple are colours I like a lot,
My **Peppa big shoes and coat** is the best present I ever got.
My favourite people are **Anita and Mummy**, who are gems,
So this, my first poem, is just for them!

Amrit Kaur (3)
Comberton Day Nursery, London

My First Poem

My name is Jorel and I go to preschool,
My best friend is my older brother, who is really cool.
I watch Thomas and Friends and Peppa Pig on TV,
Playing with my toy cars, trains and iPad is lots of fun for me.
I just love Weetabix, oats, porridge and jollof rice to eat,
And sometimes oat cakes and crisps for a treat.
Blue is a colour I like a lot,
My puzzles box and iPad are the best presents I ever got.
My favourite people are my mum and brother, who are gems,
So this, my first poem, is just for them!

Jorel Attoh Quarshie (3)
Comberton Day Nursery, London

My First Poem

My name is **Esme Young** and I go to preschool,
My best friend is **Levie**, who is really cool.
I watch **Abney and Teal and Dinosaurs** on TV,
Playing **stacking up blocks like a bridge** is lots of fun for me.
I just love **my baba's spaghetti** to eat,
And sometimes **ice cream** for a treat.
Blue is a colour I like a lot,
My **new hair bands from Santa** are the best present I ever got.
My favourite person is **Santa Claus**, who is a gem,
So this, my first poem, is just for them!

Esme Young (3)
Comberton Day Nursery, London

My First Poem

My name is **Bobby Randall** and I go to preschool,
My best friend is **Levie**, who is really cool.
I watch **Pac-Man** on TV,
Playing **digging** is lots of fun for me.
I just love **chicken** to eat,
And sometimes **cake and custard** for a treat.
Red and orange are colours I like a lot,
My **Bumblebee** is the best present I ever got.
My favourite person is **Taylor**, who is a gem,
So this, my first poem, is just for them!

Bobby Parker Randall (4)
Comberton Day Nursery, London

My First Poem

My name is Levie and I go to preschool,
My best friend is Brooke, who is really cool.
I watch Umizoomi on TV,
Playing mini Lego is lots of fun for me.
I just love chicken and chips to eat,
And sometimes sweeties and chocolate for a treat.
Blue is a colour I like a lot,
My rubber cakes are the best present I ever got.
My favourite people are Grandpa Yves and Grandma Josette, who are gems,
So this, my first poem, is just for them!

Levie Sandoz (4)
Comberton Day Nursery, London

My First Poem

My name is E'loheka and I go to preschool,
My best friend is Leona, who is really cool.
I watch Peppa Pig on TV,
Playing hide-and-seek is lots of fun for me.
I just love jollof rice to eat,
And sometimes KFC for a treat.
Pink is a colour I like a lot,
My iPad is the best present I ever got.
My favourite person is Rachel, who is a gem,
So this, my first poem, is just for them!

E'loheka Oppong-Frimpong (3)
Comberton Day Nursery, London

My First Poem

My name is Alex and I go to preschool,

My best friend is Sheil, who is really cool.

I watch Maya the Bee on TV,

Playing with my cars is lots of fun for me.

I just love cucumbers to eat,

And sometimes candy for a treat.

Blue is a colour I like a lot,

My bicycle is the best present I ever got.

My favourite person is my mom, who is a gem,

So this, my first poem, is just for them!

Alexander Nakos (3)

Comberton Day Nursery, London

My First Poem

My name is Oluwatosin and I go to preschool,
My best friend is Ashley, who is really cool.
I watch Totally Spice on TV,
Playing outside with my friends is lots of fun for me.
I just love jollof rice to eat,
And sometimes sweeties for a treat.
Purple is a colour I like a lot,
My Elsa dress is the best present I ever got.
My favourite people are Mummy and Daddy, who are gems,
So this, my first poem, is just for them!

Oluwatosin Niyi-Olowu (3)
Comberton Day Nursery, London

My First Poem

My name is Colbie and I go to preschool,
My best friend is Kyra, who is really cool.
I watch Frozen on TV,
Playing café is lots of fun for me.
I just love bananas to eat,
And sometimes sweeties for a treat.
Pink is a colour I like a lot,
My kitchen is the best present I ever got.
My favourite person is Taliah, who is a gem,
So this, my first poem, is just for them!

Colbie Marie Flower (4)
Eaton Mill Nursery, Milton Keynes

My First Poem

My name is Lena and I go to preschool,
My best friends are Alessia, Cody and Scarlet,
who are really cool.
I watch My Little Pony, Scooby-Doo
and Tom and Jerry on TV,
Playing with ponies is lots of fun for me.
I just love pasta and chicken nuggets to eat,
And sometimes a chocolate pot for a treat.
Pink and blue are colours I like a lot,
My swimming boat and castle are the best
presents I ever got.
My favourite people are Alessia, Cody, Scarlet,
Mummy and Daddy, who are gems,
So this, my first poem, is just for them!

Lena Cooper (4)
Eaton Mill Nursery, Milton Keynes

My First Poem

My name is **Warith** and I go to preschool,
My best friend is **Aiden**, who is really cool.
I watch **Nick Jr** on TV,
Playing **football** is lots of fun for me.
I just love **chips** to eat,
And sometimes **chocolate** for a treat.
Black is a colour I like a lot,
My **toy car** is the best present I ever got.
My favourite person is **Mum**, who is a gem,
So this, my first poem, is just for them!

Warith Mpalanzi (4)
Eaton Mill Nursery, Milton Keynes

My First Poem

My name is Dasia and I go to preschool,
My best friend is Paul, who is really cool.
I watch Scooby-Doo all day on TV,
Playing with Princess Anna is lots of fun for me.
I just love pancakes with Nutella to eat,
And sometimes lollipops that I get for a treat.
Sparkly pink is a colour I like a lot,
My teddy bear with purple eyes is the best present I ever got.
My favourite person is my Uncle En, who is a gem,
So this, my first poem, is just for them!

Dasia Milagros La Barbera (4)
Eaton Mill Nursery, Milton Keynes

My First Poem

My name is Reuben and I go to preschool,
My best friend is Favour, who is really cool.
I watch Pokémon on TV,
Playing on skates is lots of fun for me.
I just love curry to eat,
And sometimes ice cream for a treat.
Green is a colour I like a lot,
My motorbike is the best present I ever got.
My favourite person is Myles, who is a gem,
So this, my first poem, is just for them!

Reuben Thomas Peter Lowe (4)
Eaton Mill Nursery, Milton Keynes

My First Poem

My name is Inioluwa and I go to preschool,
My best friend is Katie, who is really cool.
I watch Frozen on TV,
Playing with babies is lots of fun for me.
I just love breadsticks to eat,
And sometimes spaghetti for a treat.
Red and orange are colours I like a lot,
My Frozen toy and tablet are the best presents
I ever got.
My favourite person is Leena, who is a gem,
So this, my first poem, is just for them!

Inioluwa Badru (3)
Eaton Mill Nursery, Milton Keynes

My First Poem

My name is Esther and I go to preschool,
My best friend is Ellis, who is really cool.
I watch Colour City on TV,
Playing Ken and Barbie is lots of fun for me.
I just love pizza to eat,
And sometimes Quavers for a treat.
Yellow is a colour I like a lot,
My Isabel doll is the best present I ever got.
My favourite person is my uncle, who is a gem,
So this, my first poem, is just for them!

Esther Aremu (4)
Eaton Mill Nursery, Milton Keynes

My First Poem

My name is Sadia and I go to preschool,
My best friends are the teachers, who are really cool.
I watch CBeebies on TV,
Playing hide-and-seek is lots of fun for me.
I just love McDonald's to eat,
And sometimes I have candy for a treat.
Purple is a colour I like a lot,
My doll's house is the best present I ever got.
My favourite person is my world, who is a gem,
So this, my first poem, is just for them!

Sadia Tasnim (4)
Eaton Mill Nursery, Milton Keynes

My First Poem

My name is Keira and I go to preschool,
My best friend is Jessica, who is really cool.
I watch Dinosaur Train on TV,
Playing in the rain is lots of fun for me.
I just love ham to eat,
And sometimes jam for a treat.
Rainbow colours are colours I like a lot,
My bike is the best present I ever got.
My favourite person is Nanny, who is a gem,
So this, my first poem, is just for them!

Keira Evelyn Simpson (4)
Eaton Mill Nursery, Milton Keynes

My First Poem

My name is **Abubakar** and I go to preschool,
My best friend is **Freddie**, who is really cool.
I watch **Andy's Prehistoric Adventures** on TV,
Playing **with my dinosaur and toy cars** is lots of fun for me.
I just love **cheese sandwiches** to eat,
And sometimes **I have cookies or chocolate** for a treat.
Brown is a colour I like a lot,
My **remote-controlled dinosaur** is the best present I ever got.
My favourite person is **my daddy**, who is a gem,
So this, my first poem, is just for them!

Abubakar Amin Yusuf (4)
Eaton Mill Nursery, Milton Keynes

My First Poem

My name is **Tolbert Kofi Agyeman** and I attend one of the best preschools in the country,
My best friend is **Israel**, who is really cool.
I watch **Subway Surf** on TV, and
Playing **pretend Subway Surf** is lots of fun for me.
I just love eating **rice pudding** because it is yummy,
And sometimes **have ice cream** for a treat.
Blue is a colour I like best
My **race car** is the best present I ever got.
My favourite person is **my baby brother**, who is a real gem,
So this, my first poem, is just for them!

Tolbert Kofi Agyeman (4)
Eaton Mill Nursery, Milton Keynes

My First Poem

My name is Ella and I go to preschool,
My best friend is Kyra, who is really cool.
I watch Peppa Pig on TV,
Playing with my Play-Doh is lots of fun for me.
I just love strawberries and grapes to eat,
And sometimes chocolate for a treat.
Pink and purple are colours I like a lot,
My bunny is the best present I ever got.
My favourite person is Raff, who is a gem,
So this, my first poem, is just for them!

Ella Stodart (3)
Eaton Mill Nursery, Milton Keynes

My First Poem

My name is **Zunairah** and I go to preschool,
My best friend is **Arfa**, who is really cool.
I watch **Tiny Pop** on TV,
Playing **with my bicycle** is lots of fun for me.
I just love **chicken and crisps** to eat,
And sometimes **I like chocolate cake** for a treat.
Blue is a colour I like a lot,
My **bicycle** is the best present I ever got.
My favourite person is **Mum**, who is a gem,
So this, my first poem, is just for them!

Zunairah Hasan (4)
Eaton Mill Nursery, Milton Keynes

My First Poem

My name is Tayah and I go to preschool,
My best friend is Olivia, who is really cool.
I watch Ben & Holly's Little Kingdom on TV,
Playing cars is lots of fun for me.
I just love peanut and jam sandwiches to eat,
And sometimes Oreos for a treat.
Blue is a colour I like a lot,
My soft toy sheep is the best present I ever got.
My favourite person is Mom, who is a gem,
So this, my first poem, is just for them!

Tayah Puchner (2)
Eaton Mill Nursery, Milton Keynes

My First Poem

My name is **Joe** and I go to preschool,
My best friend is **Kira**, who is really cool.
I watch **Peppa Pig** on TV,
Playing **Skylanders** is lots of fun for me.
I just love **bananas** to eat,
And sometimes **sweets** for a treat.
Yellow is a colour I like a lot,
My **train track** is the best present I ever got.
My favourite person is **Kira**, who is a gem,
So this, my first poem, is just for them!

Joe McNab (4)
Eaton Mill Nursery, Milton Keynes

My First Poem

My name is Ellis and I go to preschool,
My best friend is Daddy, who is really cool.
I watch football on TV,
Playing fighting with Daddy is lots of fun for me.
I just love pasta and baked beans to eat,
And sometimes salami for a treat.
Red is a colour I like a lot,
My big room is the best present I ever got.
My favourite person is Tia, my dog, who is a gem,
So this, my first poem, is just for them!

Ellis Louis John Quailey (4)
Eaton Mill Nursery, Milton Keynes

My First Poem

My name is Leo and I go to preschool,
My best friend is Evie, who is really cool.
I watch Peppa Pig on TV,
Playing with puzzles is lots of fun for me.
I just love chocolate buttons to eat,
And sometimes more of those for a treat.
Blue is a colour I like a lot,
My Peppa Pig puzzle is the best present I ever got.
My favourite person is Daddy, who is a gem,
So this, my first poem, is just for them!

Leo Segebrecht (3)
Eaton Mill Nursery, Milton Keynes

My First Poem

My name is **Fabian** and I go to preschool,
My best friend is **Tommy**, who is really cool.
I watch **PAW Patrol** on TV,
Playing **in the home corner** is lots of fun for me.
I just love **chocolate cake and milk** to eat,
And sometimes **jelly** for a treat.
Yellow and red are colours I like a lot,
My **scooter** is the best present I ever got.
My favourite people are **Mummy and Daddy**, who are gems,
So this, my first poem, is just for them!

Fabian Watts (3)
Eaton Mill Nursery, Milton Keynes

My First Poem

My name is **Ashleigh** and I go to preschool,
My best friend is **Mason**, who is really cool.
I watch **H2O Mermaid Adventures** on TV,
Playing **mermaids** is lots of fun for me.
I just love **sausage and mash** to eat,
And sometimes **some cake** for a treat.
Pink is a colour I like a lot,
My **Bunny** is the best present I ever got.
My favourite person is **Mummy**, who is a gem,
So this, my first poem, is just for them!

Ashleigh Turney-Harris (4)
Eaton Mill Nursery, Milton Keynes

My First Poem

My name is Ollie and I go to preschool,
My best friends are Jasper and Tay, who are really cool.
I watch superheroes on TV,
Playing Avengers is lots of fun for me.
I just love pasta to eat,
And sometimes Haribos for a treat.
Blue is a colour I like a lot,
My Transformers are the best present I ever got.
My favourite person is Mummy, who is a gem,
So this, my first poem, is just for them!

Ollie Ledster (4)
Eaton Mill Nursery, Milton Keynes

My First Poem

My name is **Elsie-Mae and I love to play** and I go to preschool,
My best friend is **my brother Ted and his hair is red and he** is really cool.
I watch **my mum cook and watch cartoons** on TV,
Playing **with balloons and blowing bubbles** is lots of fun for me.
I just love **cuddles and snuggles and love going out** to eat,
And sometimes **when I'm good my daddy takes me** for a treat.
I know I should like pink but blue is a colour I like a lot,
My **size 9 skates** are the best present I ever got.
My favourite person is **my brother who I love a lot**, who is a gem,
So this, my first poem, is just for them!

Elsie-Mae Daniella Barnett (3)
Eaton Mill Nursery, Milton Keynes

My First Poem

My name is Poppy-Mae and I go to preschool,
My best friend is Minnie, who is really cool.
I watch PAW Patrol on TV,
Playing Play-Doh is lots of fun for me.
I just love beans to eat,
And sometimes sweets for a treat.
Pink is a colour I like a lot,
My Barbie is the best present I ever got.
My favourite person is Chelsie, who is a gem,
So this, my first poem, is just for them!

Poppy-Mae Mintram (3)
Eaton Mill Nursery, Milton Keynes

My First Poem

My name is **Kira** and I go to preschool,
My best friend is **Colby**, who is really cool.
I watch **Frozen** on TV,
Playing **on my trampoline** is lots of fun for me.
I just love **chicken nuggets** to eat,
And sometimes **chocolate** for a treat.
Red is a colour I like a lot,
My **doll's house** is the best present I ever got.
My favourite person is **Mummy**, who is a gem,
So this, my first poem, is just for them!

Kira Morris (4)
Eaton Mill Nursery, Milton Keynes

My First Poem

My name is **Tillie** and I go to preschool,
My best friend is **Elsie-Mae**, who is really cool.
I watch **Maco Mermaids** on TV,
Playing **hopscotch** is lots of fun for me.
I just love **jelly and ice cream** to eat,
And sometimes **sweeties** for a treat.
Pink is a colour I like a lot,
My **dolls** are the best present I ever got.
My favourite person is **Lacie**, who is a gem,
So this, my first poem, is just for them!

Tillie James (4)
Eaton Mill Nursery, Milton Keynes

My First Poem

My name is Freddie and I go to preschool,
My best friend is Ellis, who is really cool.
I watch Mr Bean on TV,
Playing with Lego is lots of fun for me.
I just love mash and gravy to eat,
And sometimes ice cream for a treat.
Red is a colour I like a lot,
My bike is the best present I ever got.
My favourite person is my mummy, who is a gem,
So this, my first poem, is just for them!

Freddie Keep (4)
Eaton Mill Nursery, Milton Keynes

My First Poem

My name is Richard and I go to preschool,
My best friend is Tyler, who is really cool.
I watch Blaze and the Monster Machines
on TV,
Playing racing cars is lots of fun for me.
I just love noodles to eat,
And sometimes orange juice for a treat.
Red is a colour I like a lot,
My police car is the best present I ever got.
My favourite person is Mummy, who is a gem,
So this, my first poem, is just for them!

Richard Abioye (3)
Eaton Mill Nursery, Milton Keynes

My First Poem

My name is Lotti and I go to preschool,
My best friend is Francis, who is really cool.
I watch PAW Patrol on TV,
Playing babies is lots of fun for me.
I just love chips and beans to eat,
And sometimes McDonald's for a treat.
Pink is a colour I like a lot,
My bike is the best present I ever got.
My favourite person is Chloe, who is a gem,
So this, my first poem, is just for them!

Lotti Perry (2)
Eaton Mill Nursery, Milton Keynes

My First Poem

My name is David and I go to preschool,
My best friend is my cousin, Helena, who is really cool.
I watch Jake and the Neverland Pirates on TV,
Playing on drums and football is lots of fun for me.
I just love lasagne to eat,
And sometimes a Kinder Surprise for a treat.
Blue is a colour I like a lot,
My drum is the best present I ever got.
My favourite people are my mum and my dad, who are gems,
So this, my first poem, is just for them!

David Bruno Carneiro Ferreira (3)
Eaton Mill Nursery, Milton Keynes

My First Poem

My name is Mia and I go to preschool,
My best friend is Kira, who is really cool.
I watch PAW Patrol on TV,
Playing on my trampoline is lots of fun for me.
I just love sausages to eat,
And sometimes ice cream for a treat.
Black is a colour I like a lot,
My doll's house is the best present I ever got.
My favourite person is Mummy, who is a gem,
So this, my first poem, is just for them!

Mia Hurst (4)
Eaton Mill Nursery, Milton Keynes

My First Poem

My name is **Francis Ellen Ridge** and I go to preschool,
My best friends are **Lottie and Drew**, who are really cool.
I watch **Umizoomi and Ghostbusters** on TV,
Playing **teddies** is lots of fun for me.
I just love **spaghetti Bolognese** to eat,
And sometimes **strawberry cake** for a treat.
Green is a colour I like a lot,
My **little baby brother** is the best present I ever got.
My favourite person is **Kurtis, my brother**, who is a gem,
So this, my first poem, is just for them!

Francis Ellen Ridge (3)
Eaton Mill Nursery, Milton Keynes

My First Poem

My name is Leo and I go to preschool,

My best friend is Corey, who is really cool.

I watch Fireman Sam, Paw Patrol and Blaze on TV,

Playing cars and trains is lots of fun for me.

I just love pizza and chips to eat,

And sometimes we have ice cream for a treat.

Blue is a colour I like a lot,

My iPad is the best present I ever got.

My favourite person is my mum, who is a gem,

So this, my first poem, is just for them!

Leo Charles Marlow (4)

Eaton Mill Nursery, Milton Keynes

My First Poem

My name is Skye and I go to preschool,
My best friend is Riley, who is really cool.
I watch Peppa Pig on TV,
Playing with puzzles is lots of fun for me.
I just love chicken and pizza to eat,
And sometimes a Kinder egg for a treat.
Red is a colour I like a lot,
My Toy Story characters are the best present I ever got.
My favourite person is Mummy, who is a gem,
So this, my first poem, is just for them!

Skye Gillian Johnson (3)
Eaton Mill Nursery, Milton Keynes

My First Poem

My name is Mylah Biscoe and I go to preschool,
My best friend is Sky, who is really cool.
I watch The Hive on TV,
Playing doctors with Bruce is lots of fun for me.
I just love pasta with green sauce or soup to eat,
And sometimes chocolate for a treat.
Purple and blue are colours I like a lot,
My bike and scooter are the best presents I ever got.
My favourite person is Hallé, my sister, who is a gem,
So this, my first poem, is just for them!

Mylah Biscoe (3)
Eaton Mill Nursery, Milton Keynes

My First Poem

My name is Samuel and I go to preschool,
My best friend is Kyra, who is really cool.
I watch PAW Patrol on TV,
Playing cars is lots of fun for me.
I just love pears to eat,
And sometimes chocolate for a treat.
Orange is a colour I like a lot,
My animals are the best present I ever got.
My favourite person is G, who is a gem,
So this, my first poem, is just for them!

Samuel Brindle (2)
Eaton Mill Nursery, Milton Keynes

My First Poem

My name is Callum and I go to preschool,
My best friend is Jasper, who is really cool.
I watch Gumball on TV,
Playing Mario is lots of fun for me.
I just love chicken to eat,
And sometimes I have chocolate cake for a treat.
White is a colour I like a lot,
My Nintendo DS is the best present I ever got.
My favourite person is Ellis, who is a gem,
So this, my first poem, is just for them!

Callum Michael Mendes O'Brien (4)
Eaton Mill Nursery, Milton Keynes

My First Poem

My name is Jasper and I go to preschool,
My best friend is Israel, who is really cool.
I watch Scooby-Doo on TV,
Playing with Mouse Trap is lots of fun for me.
I just love hot dogs and chips to eat,
And sometimes a chocolate bar for a treat.
Pink and blue are colours I like a lot,
My remote-controlled car is the best present I ever got.
My favourite person is Mummy, who is a gem,
So this, my first poem, is just for them!

Jasper Beddall (4)
Eaton Mill Nursery, Milton Keynes

My First Poem

My name is **Henry** and I go to preschool,
My best friend is **Mummy**, who is really cool.
I watch **Blaze** on TV,
Playing **lorries** is lots of fun for me.
I just love **cheese and sausages** to eat,
And sometimes **sweets** for a treat.
Purple is a colour I like a lot,
My **Thunderbirds** are the best present I ever got.
My favourite person is **Mummy**, who is a gem,
So this, my first poem, is just for them!

Henry Williams (3)
Eaton Mill Nursery, Milton Keynes

My First Poem

My name is **Zayyan** and I go to preschool,
My best friend is **Callam**, who is really cool.
I watch **Ben 10** on TV,
Playing **superheroes** is lots of fun for me.
I just love **cheese** to eat,
And sometimes **chocolate yoghurt** for a treat.
Red is a colour I like a lot,
My **toy truck** is the best present I ever got.
My favourite person is **my big sister**, who is a gem,
So this, my first poem, is just for them!

Zayyan Anwar Miah (3)
Eaton Mill Nursery, Milton Keynes

My First Poem

My name is **Yunus** and I go to preschool,
My best friend is **Ayyub**, who is really cool.
I watch **Power Rangers** on TV,
Playing **with dinosaurs and cars** is lots of fun for me.
I just love **egg, bread, cake and beans** to eat,
And sometimes **sweets and ice cream** for a treat.
Blue, red and green are colours I like a lot,
My **Superman costume** is the best present I ever got.
My favourite people are **my mum, dad and sister**, who are gems,
So this, my first poem, is just for them!

Yunus Hussain (3)
Eaton Mill Nursery, Milton Keynes

My First Poem

My name is **Nico** and I go to preschool,
My best friend is **Tommy**, who is really cool.
I watch **Pokémon** on TV,
Playing **catch** is lots of fun for me.
I just love **fish** to eat,
And sometimes **chocolate** for a treat.
Red is a colour I like a lot,
My **bike** is the best present I ever got.
My favourite person is **Andres**, who is a gem,
So this, my first poem, is just for them!

Nico Rutter (5)
Eaton Mill Nursery, Milton Keynes

My First Poem

My name is **Charlotte Butler** and I go to preschool,
My best friend is **Julie (my teacher)**, who is really cool.
I watch **PAW Patrol and CBBC** on TV,
Playing **outside with my friends** is lots of fun for me.
I just love **grapes and bananas** to eat,
And sometimes **chocolate and crisps** for a treat.
Pink is a colour I like a lot,
My **Kindle Fire** is the best present I ever got.
My favourite people are **my nanny and grandad**, who are gems,
So this, my first poem, is just for them!

Charlotte Butler (3)
Eaton Mill Nursery, Milton Keynes

My First Poem

My name is Bonnie and I go to preschool,
My best friends are Kyla and Layla, who are really cool.
I watch PAW Patrol on TV,
Playing with my PAW Patrol toys is lots of fun for me.
I just love cucumber and cheese to eat,
And sometimes chocolate for a treat.
Red is a colour I like a lot,
My Marshall dress is the best present I ever got.
My favourite person is Nanny, who is a gem,
So this, my first poem, is just for them!

Bonnie Jae Hurst (3)
Eaton Mill Nursery, Milton Keynes

My First Poem

My name is **Sophie** and I go to preschool,
My best friend is **Tilly**, who is really cool.
I watch **Bubble Guppies and Peppa Pig** on TV,
Playing **snakes and ladders** is lots of fun for me.
I just love **noodles and roast chicken** to eat,
And sometimes **ice cream and chocolate** for a treat.
Pink is a colour I like a lot,
My **Frozen toys** are the best present I ever got.
My favourite person is **Nanny**, who is a gem,
So this, my first poem, is just for them!

Sophie Faulkner (4)
Eaton Mill Nursery, Milton Keynes

My First Poem

My name is Fearne and I go to preschool,
My best friend is Lola, who is really cool.
I watch Topsy and Tim on TV,
Playing hide-and-seek is lots of fun for me.
I just love strawberries to eat,
And sometimes crisps for a treat.
Pink is a colour I like a lot,
My Minnie Mouse is the best present I ever got.
My favourite person is Mummy, who is a gem,
So this, my first poem, is just for them!

Fearne Cowie (3)
Eaton Mill Nursery, Milton Keynes

My First Poem

My name is **Daniel** and I go to preschool,
My best friend is **Asia**, who is really cool.
I watch **Frozen Elsa** on TV,
Playing **with cars** is lots of fun for me.
I just love **bread** to eat,
And sometimes **chocolate** for a treat.
Red is a colour I like a lot,
My **jingle bells** are the best present I ever got.
My favourite people are **Daddy and Mummy**, who are gems,
So this, my first poem, is just for them!

Daniel Andrei Cosovat (4)
Fellowship House Children's Centre, London

My First Poem

My name is Olivia and I go to preschool,
My best friend is Mya, who is really cool.
I watch Peppa Pig on TV,
Playing George Pig is lots of fun for me.
I just love sandwiches to eat,
And sometimes ice cream for a treat.
Blue is a colour I like a lot,
My Jessie is the best present I ever got.
My favourite person is Mummy, who is a gem,
So this, my first poem, is just for them!

Olivia Warren (2)
Happy Valley Preschool, Newhaven

My First Poem

My name is Bella and I go to preschool,
My best friend is Mia, who is really cool.
I watch Mickey Mouse on TV,
Playing Play-Doh is lots of fun for me.
I just love pink Pringles to eat,
And sometimes chocolate for a treat.
Pink is a colour I like a lot,
My dinosaur is the best present I ever got.
My favourite person is Bethany, who is a gem,
So this, my first poem, is just for them!

Isabella Deacon (3)
Happy Valley Preschool, Newhaven

My First Poem

My name is Connor and I go to preschool,
My best friend is Luka, who is really cool.
I watch Spider-Man on TV,
Playing Xbox games is lots of fun for me.
I just love chocolate spread to eat,
And sometimes biscuits for a treat.
Blue is a colour I like a lot,
My Spider-Man is the best present I ever got.
My favourite people are Daddy and Mummy, who are gems,
So this, my first poem, is just for them!

Connor Pryor (4)
Happy Valley Preschool, Newhaven

My First Poem

My name is Sophie and I go to preschool,
My best friend is Mia, who is really cool.
I watch Peppa Pig on TV,
Playing Daddy's Kindle Fire is lots of fun for me.
I just love chocolate to eat,
And sometimes fruit stars for a treat.
Red is a colour I like a lot,
My slide is the best present I ever got.
My favourite person is my teddy, who is a gem,
So this, my first poem, is just for them!

Sophie Walker (2)
Happy Valley Preschool, Newhaven

My First Poem

My name is Mia and I go to preschool,
My best friend is Max, who is really cool.
I watch Peppa Pig on TV,
Playing wrestling is lots of fun for me.
I just love spaghetti Bolognese to eat,
And sometimes ice cream for a treat.
Blue is a colour I like a lot,
My trampoline is the best present I ever got.
My favourite person is Shaun, who is a gem,
So this, my first poem, is just for them!

Mia Deacon (3)
Happy Valley Preschool, Newhaven

My First Poem

My name is **Charlie** and I go to preschool,
My best friend is **Tommy**, who is really cool.
I watch **Peppa Pig** on TV,
Playing **Ben 10** is lots of fun for me.
I just love **burgers and ketchup** to eat,
And sometimes **sweeties** for a treat.
Blue is a colour I like a lot,
My **teddy** is the best present I ever got.
My favourite person is **Mummy**, who is a gem,
So this, my first poem, is just for them!

Charlie Bassett (3)
Happy Valley Preschool, Newhaven

My First Poem

My name is Tommy and I go to preschool,
My best friend is Max, who is really cool.
I watch Star Wars on TV,
Playing with Kasey is lots of fun for me.
I just love biscuits to eat,
And sometimes a Kinder egg for a treat.
Blue is a colour I like a lot,
My Iron Man hand is the best present I ever got.
My favourite person is Iron man, who is a gem,
So this, my first poem, is just for them!

Tommy Bentley (4)
Happy Valley Preschool, Newhaven

My First Poem

My name is Ashleigh and I go to preschool,
My best friend is Lexi-Elisse, who is really cool.
I watch Simpsons on TV,
Playing dollies is lots of fun for me.
I just love noodles to eat,
And sometimes sweets for a treat.
Blue is a colour I like a lot,
My Baby Annabell is the best present I ever got.
My favourite people are Mummy and Daddy, who are gems,
So this, my first poem, is just for them!

Ashleigh Streatfield-Mollon (4)
Happy Valley Preschool, Newhaven

My First Poem

My name is Becky and I go to preschool,
My best friend is Max, who is really cool.
I watch Peppa Pig on TV,
Playing trains is lots of fun for me.
I just love lemons to eat,
And sometimes cookies for a treat.
Blue is a colour I like a lot,
My teddy is the best present I ever got.
My favourite person is Lilly-Mae, who is a gem,
So this, my first poem, is just for them!

Becky Hector (3)
Happy Valley Preschool, Newhaven

My First Poem

My name is Lexi and I go to preschool,
My best friend is Harvey, who is really cool.
I watch Peppa Pig on TV,
Playing with Peppa Pig is lots of fun for me.
I just love cheese to eat,
And sometimes chocolate for a treat.
Blue is a colour I like a lot,
My drawing set is the best present I ever got.
My favourite person is Nannie, who is a gem,
So this, my first poem, is just for them!

Lexi Cranmer (4)
Happy Valley Preschool, Newhaven

My First Poem

My name is Luka and I go to preschool,
My best friend is Connor, who is really cool.
I watch Batman on TV,
Playing Action Men is lots of fun for me.
I just love fish, chips and burgers to eat,
And sometimes chocolate buttons for a treat.
Red and blue are colours I like a lot,
My Transformer Batcave is the best present I ever got.
My favourite person is Superman, who is a gem,
So this, my first poem, is just for them!

Luka Lambert (4)
Happy Valley Preschool, Newhaven

My First Poem

My name is Max and I go to preschool,
My best friend is Tommy, who is really cool.
I watch Batman on TV,
Playing driving Batman's car is lots of fun for me.
I just love bacon, potato and fish fingers to eat,
And sometimes a KitKat for a treat.
Blue and orange are colours I like a lot,
My Buzz Lightyear is the best present I ever got.
My favourite person is Mickey Mouse, who is a gem,
So this, my first poem, is just for them!

Max Huggett (4)
Happy Valley Preschool, Newhaven

My First Poem

My name is Mya and I go to preschool,

My best friend is Little Lexi, who is really cool.

I watch Spot Box on TV,

Playing babies is lots of fun for me.

I just love pasta to eat,

And sometimes ice cream for a treat.

Blue is a colour I like a lot,

My doll is the best present I ever got.

My favourite person is Daddy, who is a gem,

So this, my first poem, is just for them!

Mya Ridgway (3)
Happy Valley Preschool, Newhaven

My First Poem

My name is **Lexi-Elisse** and I go to preschool,
My best friends are **Ashleigh and Aleah**, who are really cool.
I watch **PAW Patrol** on TV,
Playing **PAW Patrol colouring** is lots of fun for me.
I just love **carrot sticks** to eat,
And sometimes **cucumber** for a treat.
Blue and red are colours I like a lot,
My **Baby Annabell** is the best present I ever got.
My favourite person is **Nana**, who is a gem,
So this, my first poem, is just for them!

Lexi-Elisse Bowles (4)

Happy Valley Preschool, Newhaven

My First Poem

My name is **Paige-Summer** and I go to preschool,
My best friend is **Jamie**, who is really cool.
I watch **Ben & Holly's Little Kingdom** on TV,
Playing **toy horse** is lots of fun for me.
I just love **spaghetti Bolognese** to eat,
And sometimes **making cakes** for a treat.
Red is a colour I like a lot,
My **squeaky toy** is the best present I ever got.
My favourite person is **Max**, who is a gem,
So this, my first poem, is just for them!

Paige-Summer Greaney (3)
Happy Valley Preschool, Newhaven

My First Poem

My name is Lilly-Mae and I go to preschool,
My best friend is Ocean, who is really cool.
I watch a giraffe on TV,
Playing babies is lots of fun for me.
I just love toast to eat,
And sometimes chocolate for a treat.
Blue is a colour I like a lot,
My iPad is the best present I ever got.
My favourite person is Poppy-Mae, who is a gem,
So this, my first poem, is just for them!

Lilly-Mae Dewdney (4)
Happy Valley Preschool, Newhaven

My First Poem

My name is Jamie-Sienna and I go to preschool,
My best friend is Jack, who is really cool.
I watch Ben & Holly's Little Kingdom on TV,
Playing dolls is lots of fun for me.
I just love eggs to eat,
And sometimes biscuits for a treat.
Black is a colour I like a lot,
My horse is the best present I ever got.
My favourite person is Daddy, who is a gem,
So this, my first poem, is just for them!

Jamie-Sienna Greaney (2)
Happy Valley Preschool, Newhaven

My First Poem

My name is Ocean and I go to preschool,
My best friend is Harry, who is really cool.
I watch Mr Tumble on TV,
Playing with a bunny rabbit is lots of fun for me.
I just love chocolate spread sandwiches to eat,
And sometimes crisps for a treat.
Red is a colour I like a lot,
My dinosaur is the best present I ever got.
My favourite person is Mummy, who is a gem,
So this, my first poem, is just for them!

Ocean Ridgway (4)
Happy Valley Preschool, Newhaven

My First Poem

My name is Emre and I go to preschool,
My best friend is Asyia, who is really cool.
I watch PAW Patrol on TV,
Playing dinosaurs is lots of fun for me.
I just love jacket potato to eat,
And sometimes Chinese for a treat.
Blue is a colour I like a lot,
My Buzz Lightyear is the best present I ever got.
My favourite person is Baba, who is a gem,
So this, my first poem, is just for them!

Emre Endogan (3)
Happy Valley Preschool, Newhaven

My First Poem

My name is Alex and I go to preschool,
My best friend is Olivia, who is really cool.
I watch Peppa Pig and Bing on TV,
Playing cars and trains is lots of fun for me.
I just love food - all sorts to eat,
And sometimes chocolate for a treat.
Purple and red are colours I like a lot,
My Iggle Piggle and Bing teddy are the best presents I ever got.
My favourite people are my brothers, Tommy and Kasey, who are gems,
So this, my first poem, is just for them!

Alexander Bentley (2)
Happy Valley Preschool, Newhaven

My First Poem

My name is Aleah and I go to preschool,
My best friend is Lexi, who is really cool.
I watch PJ Mast on TV,
Playing with building blocks is lots of fun for me.
I just love chocolate spread on toast to eat,
And sometimes lollipops for a treat.
Pink is a colour I like a lot,
My Cinderella dress is the best present I ever got.
My favourite person is Mummy, who is a gem,
So this, my first poem, is just for them!

Aleah-Louise Bowles-Taplin (4)
Happy Valley Preschool, Newhaven

My First Poem

My name is Jackson and I go to preschool,
My best friend is Mathew, who is really cool.
I watch Spider-Man on TV,
Playing with my tractors is lots of fun for me.
I just love egg sandwiches to eat,
And sometimes sweeties for a treat.
Green is a colour I like a lot,
My John Deere tractor is the best present I ever got.
My favourite person is Grandad Dessie, who is a gem,
So this, my first poem, is just for them!

Jackson McKee (4)
Little Friends Preschool, Banbridge

My First Poem

My name is Anna and I go to preschool,
My best friend is Oscar, who is really cool.
I watch Numtums on TV,
Playing with Lego is lots of fun for me.
I just love top hats to eat,
And sometimes ice cream for a treat.
Pink is a colour I like a lot,
My Pinkie Pie is the best present I ever got.
My favourite person is Mum, who is a gem,
So this, my first poem, is just for them!

Anna Parkes (4)
Little Friends Preschool, Banbridge

My First Poem

My name is **Jayden** and I go to preschool,
My best friend is **Ethan**, who is really cool.
I watch **PAW Patrol** on TV,
Playing **with my toys and outside** is lots of fun for me.
I just love **bagels and strawberries** to eat,
And sometimes **sweeties** for a treat.
Blue is a colour I like a lot,
My **big sit-on tractor** is the best present I ever got.
My favourite person is **my little brother, Connor**, who is a gem,
So this, my first poem, is just for them!

Jayden Campbell (3)
Little Friends Preschool, Banbridge

My First Poem

My name is **Juliana Nelson** and I go to preschool,
My best friend is **Eabha**, who is really cool.
I watch **Horseland** on TV,
Playing **with my dog Sasha** is lots of fun for me.
I just love **spicy ribs** to eat,
And sometimes **an ice lolly** for a treat.
Purple is a colour I like a lot,
My **pony, Star,** is the best present I ever got.
My favourite person is **Daddy**, who is a gem,
So this, my first poem, is just for them!

Juliana Rachel Nelson (4)
Little Friends Preschool, Banbridge

My First Poem

My name is **Lucy** and I go to preschool,
My best friend is **Nora**, who is really cool.
I watch **Frozen** on TV,
Playing **Lego** is lots of fun for me.
I just love **sweeties** to eat,
And sometimes **an Easter egg** for a treat.
Pink is a colour I like a lot,
My **princess dolly** is the best present I ever got.
My favourite person is **dolly**, who is a gem,
So this, my first poem, is just for them!

Lucy Black (4)
Little Friends Preschool, Banbridge

My First Poem

My name is Alexandra, my mum calls me Cookems and I go to preschool,
My best friend is Joe Joe, who is really cool.
I watch Peppa Pig on TV,
Playing with my brother Nathan is lots of fun for me.
I just love bananas, spaghetti Bolognese and all my mum's cooking to eat,
And sometimes my dad fills up the crisp bowl for a treat.
Pink is a colour I like a lot,
My little crazy cart is the best present I ever got.
My favourite people are all my family, who are gems,
So this, my first poem, is just for them!

Alexandra Davidson (4)
Little Friends Preschool, Banbridge

My First Poem

My name is **Alfie** and I go to preschool,
My best friend is **Ryan**, who is really cool.
I watch **Ninja Turtles** on TV,
Playing **football** is lots of fun for me.
I just love **spaghetti hoops** to eat,
And sometimes **chocolate buttons** for a treat.
Green is a colour I like a lot,
My **bike** is the best present I ever got.
My favourite person is **Daddy**, who is a gem,
So this, my first poem, is just for them!

Alfie Moore (4)
Little Friends Preschool, Banbridge

My First Poem

My name is Ethan and I go to preschool,
My best friend is Brogan, who is really cool.
I watch Lightning McQueen on TV,
Playing cars is lots of fun for me.
I just love blue ice cream to eat,
And sometimes hot chocolate with marshmallows for a treat.
Blue is a colour I like a lot,
My police bike is the best present I ever got.
My favourite people are Mummy, Daddy and Rhys,
who are gems,
So this, my first poem, is just for them!

Ethan Young (4)
Little Friends Preschool, Banbridge

My First Poem

My name is **Brogan** and I go to preschool,
My best friend is **Josh**, who is really cool.
I watch **Lego men** on TV,
Playing **building Lego** is lots of fun for me.
I just love **sausage and beans** to eat,
And sometimes **burger sweets** for a treat.
Red is a colour I like a lot,
My **Batman** is the best present I ever got.
My favourite person is **Mummy**, who is a gem,
So this, my first poem, is just for them!

Brogan Malone (4)
Little Friends Preschool, Banbridge

My First Poem

My name is **Masen** and I go to preschool,
My best friend is **Emily**, who is really cool.
I watch **Peppa Pig** on TV,
Playing **with the big Lego** is lots of fun for me.
I just love **crackers, ham and cheese** to eat,
And sometimes **Maltesers** for a treat.
Blue is a colour I like a lot,
My **jigsaw** is the best present I ever got.
My favourite person is **Granny Helen**, who is a gem,
So this, my first poem, is just for them!

Masen Paul McKiverigan-Thompson (3)
Little Friends Preschool, Banbridge

My First Poem

My name is Katie and I go to preschool,
My best friend is Alexandra, who is really cool.
I watch Blaze and the Monster Machines on TV,
Playing in the sandpit is lots of fun for me.
I just love fish fingers to eat,
And sometimes jelly babies for a treat.
Pink is a colour I like a lot,
My Elsa singing doll is the best present I ever got.
My favourite person is Daddy, who is a gem,
So this, my first poem, is just for them!

Katie McKnight (3)
Little Friends Preschool, Banbridge

My First Poem

My name is **Matthew King** and I go to preschool,
My best friend is **Isaac**, who is really cool.
I watch **Gold Rush with my daddy** on TV,
Playing **tractors and building sites** is lots of fun for me.
I just love **wraps, fish fingers, cheese and chocolate** to eat,
And sometimes **sweets and ice lollies** for a treat.
Green is a colour I like a lot,
My **silage harvester** is the best present I ever got.
My favourite person is **Daddy**, who is a gem,
So this, my first poem, is just for them!

Matthew King (4)
Little Friends Preschool, Banbridge

My First Poem

My name is **Isaac William** and I go to preschool,
My best friend is **my cousin, Angus**, who is really cool.
I watch **Peppa Pig** on TV,
Playing **with my big blue New Holland tractor** is lots of fun for me.
I just love **pepperoni pizza** to eat,
And sometimes **vanilla ice cream** for a treat.
Blue is a colour I like a lot,
My **big wooden farm** is the best present I ever got.
My favourite person is **my mummy**, who is a gem,
So this, my first poem, is just for them!

Isaac William Mathers (4)
Little Friends Preschool, Banbridge

My First Poem

My name is **Benjamin** and I go to preschool,
My best friend is **Lorrin**, who is really cool.
I watch **Red and Grey** on TV,
Playing **xylophone** is lots of fun for me.
I just love **onions** to eat,
And sometimes **hi five** for a treat.
Blue is a colour I like a lot,
My **elephant** is the best present I ever got.
My favourite person is **Mummy**, who is a gem,
So this, my first poem, is just for them!

Benjamin Rafferty
Little House Day Nursery & Preschool, London

My First Poem

My name is Samora and I go to preschool,
My best friend is Olivia, who is really cool.
I watch Mickey Mouse on TV,
Playing blocks is lots of fun for me.
I just love spaghetti to eat,
And sometimes the book 'Sleeping Bunny' for a treat.
Pink is a colour I like a lot,
My magic mirror is the best present I ever got.
My favourite person is Daddy, who is a gem,
So this, my first poem, is just for them!

Samora Banda (3)
Little House Day Nursery & Preschool, London

My First Poem

My name is **Rayea** and I go to preschool,
My best friend is **Angelina**, who is really cool.
I watch **Peter Rabbit** on TV,
Playing **with the shape boards** is lots of fun for me.
I just love **chicken soup** to eat,
And sometimes **chocolate** for a treat.
Pink and blue are colours I like a lot,
My **Topsy and Hedgehog** are the best presents I ever got.
My favourite person is **Nana**, who is a gem,
So this, my first poem, is just for them!

Rayea Anastasia Scott (2)
Little House Day Nursery & Preschool, London

My First Poem

My name is **Henry** and I go to preschool,
My best friend is **Thomas L**, who is really cool.
I watch **Star Wars** on TV,
Playing **cars** is lots of fun for me.
I just love **sausage and fish fingers** to eat,
And sometimes **sweeties** for a treat.
Blue is a colour I like a lot,
My **Lego cars** are the best present I ever got.
My favourite person is **Kayano**, who is a gem,
So this, my first poem, is just for them!

Henry Scully
Little House Day Nursery & Preschool, London

My First Poem: I Love You, Daddy!

My name is Olivia and I go to preschool,
My best friend is Monty, who is really cool.
I watch CBeebies on TV,
Playing with my brother is lots of fun for me.
I just love pasta pesto to eat,
And sometimes chocolate coins for a treat.
Green is a colour I like a lot,
My toys are the best present I ever got.
My favourite person is Daddy, who is a gem,
So this, my first poem, is just for them!

Olivia Rayfield (3)
Little House Day Nursery & Preschool, London

My First Poem

My name is Victor and I go to preschool,
My best friend is Marcos, who is really cool.
I watch White Snake on TV,
Playing in the sand is lots of fun for me.
I just love fish to eat,
And sometimes chocolate for a treat.
Black is a colour I like a lot,
My tiger is the best present I ever got.
My favourite person is Marcos, who is a gem,
So this, my first poem, is just for them!

Victor Bacher
Little House Day Nursery & Preschool, London

My First Poem

My name is Filippo and I go to preschool,
My best friend is Marcos, who is really cool.
I watch Mr Tumble on TV,
Playing with cars is lots of fun for me.
I just love a big fish finger to eat,
And sometimes chocolate for a treat.
Black is a colour I like a lot,
My PAW Patrol toy is the best present I ever got.
My favourite person is Marcos, who is a gem,
So this, my first poem, is just for them!

Filippo Thomas Monetto (3)
Little House Day Nursery & Preschool, London

My First Poem

My name is Livia and I go to preschool,
My best friend is Angelina, who is really cool.
I watch Peppa Pig on TV,
Playing with sand is lots of fun for me.
I just love pasta to eat,
And sometimes oranges and sweets for a treat.
Pink is a colour I like a lot,
My dolly and kitchen toy are the best presents I ever got.
My favourite person is Daddy, who is a gem,
So this, my first poem, is just for them!

Livia
Little House Day Nursery & Preschool, London

My First Poem

My name is **James** and I go to preschool,
My best friend is **Henry**, who is really cool.
I watch **PAW Patrol** on TV,
Playing **trains** is lots of fun for me.
I just love **toast** to eat,
And sometimes **ice cream** for a treat.
Purple is a colour I like a lot,
My **light Lego** is the best present I ever got.
My favourite people are **Mummy and Daddy**, who are gems,
So this, my first poem, is just for them!

James Jaswal (4)
Little Rascals Nurseries, Tunbridge Wells

My First Poem

My name is Ava and I go to preschool,
My best friend is Matilda, who is really cool.
I watch Elsa on TV,
Playing mummies is lots of fun for me.
I just love custard to eat,
And sometimes spaghetti for a treat.
Pink is a colour I like a lot,
My brother is the best present I ever got.
My favourite person is Cooper, who is a gem,
So this, my first poem, is just for them!

Ava Cannacott (3)
Little Rascals Nurseries, Tunbridge Wells

My First Poem

My name is **Isla** and I go to preschool,
My best friend is **Jack**, who is really cool.
I watch **Frozen** on TV,
Playing **cars** is lots of fun for me.
I just love **pasta** to eat,
And sometimes **jelly** for a treat.
Pink is a colour I like a lot,
My **sewing** is the best present I ever got.
My favourite person is **Mummy**, who is a gem,
So this, my first poem, is just for them!

Isla Bysouth (4)
Little Rascals Nurseries, Tunbridge Wells

My First Poem

My name is Claire and I go to preschool,
My best friend is Jessica, who is really cool.
I watch Peppa Pig on TV,
Playing dressing up is lots of fun for me.
I just love chips to eat,
And sometimes Smarties for a treat.
Pink is a colour I like a lot,
My baby is the best present I ever got.
My favourite person is Megan, who is a gem,
So this, my first poem, is just for them!

Claire Hubbard (3)
Little Rascals Nurseries, Tunbridge Wells

My First Poem

My name is Leo and I go to preschool,

My best friend is Noah, who is really cool.

I watch Spider-Man on TV,

Playing PAW Patrol is lots of fun for me.

I just love pasta to eat,

And sometimes ice cream for a treat.

Purple is a colour I like a lot,

My superhero is the best present I ever got.

My favourite person is Mummy, who is a gem,

So this, my first poem, is just for them!

Leo Heathcoat (4)
Little Rascals Nurseries, Tunbridge Wells

My First Poem

My name is Noah and I go to preschool,
My best friend is Thomas, who is really cool.
I watch Cars on TV,
Playing racing is lots of fun for me.
I just love pizza to eat,
And sometimes sweets for a treat.
Red is a colour I like a lot,
My tractor is the best present I ever got.
My favourite person is Daddy, who is a gem,
So this, my first poem, is just for them!

Noah Swaffield-Robinson (4)
Little Rascals Nurseries, Tunbridge Wells

My First Poem

My name is Henry and I go to preschool,
My best friend is Leo, who is really cool.
I watch PAW Patrol on TV,
Playing cat boy is lots of fun for me.
I just love chicken nuggets to eat,
And sometimes chocolate for a treat.
Red is a colour I like a lot,
My tower is the best present I ever got.
My favourite person is Mummy, who is a gem,
So this, my first poem, is just for them!

Henry James Shepherd (4)
Little Rascals Nurseries, Tunbridge Wells

My First Poem

My name is Evie and I go to preschool,
My best friend is Jack, who is really cool.
I watch Dora on TV,
Playing kitchens is lots of fun for me.
I just love pizza to eat,
And sometimes chocolate for a treat.
Red is a colour I like a lot,
My baby is the best present I ever got.
My favourite person is Mummy, who is a gem,
So this, my first poem, is just for them!

Evie Simpson (3)
Little Rascals Nurseries, Tunbridge Wells

My First Poem

My name is Jack and I go to preschool,
My best friend is Noah, who is really cool.
I watch Bolt on TV,
Playing Star Wars is lots of fun for me.
I just love pasta to eat,
And sometimes custard for a treat.
Green is a colour I like a lot,
My Lego is the best present I ever got.
My favourite person is Mummy, who is a gem,
So this, my first poem, is just for them!

Jack Levett (4)
Little Rascals Nurseries, Tunbridge Wells

My First Poem

My name is Marcy and I go to preschool,
My best friend is Matilda, who is really cool.
I watch Tinkerbell on TV,
Playing with toys is lots of fun for me.
I just love peas to eat,
And sometimes chocolate for a treat.
Purple is a colour I like a lot,
My teddy is the best present I ever got.
My favourite person is Mummy, who is a gem,
So this, my first poem, is just for them!

Marcy Winter (3)
Little Rascals Nurseries, Tunbridge Wells

My First Poem

My name is Holden and I go to preschool,
My best friend is Noah, who is really cool.
I watch Peppa Pig on TV,
Playing Hungry Hippos is lots of fun for me.
I just love chilli to eat,
And sometimes cookies for a treat.
Orange is a colour I like a lot,
My Lego is the best present I ever got.
My favourite person is Mummy, who is a gem,
So this, my first poem, is just for them!

Holden Nouyou (4)
Little Rascals Nurseries, Tunbridge Wells

My First Poem

My name is Finlay and I go to preschool,
My best friend is Hugo, who is really cool.
I watch Star Wars on TV,
Playing Lego is lots of fun for me.
I just love pizza to eat,
And sometimes yoghurt for a treat.
Red is a colour I like a lot,
My train is the best present I ever got.
My favourite person is Daddy, who is a gem,
So this, my first poem, is just for them!

Finlay Evans (4)
Little Rascals Nurseries, Tunbridge Wells

My First Poem

My name is Joshua and I go to preschool,
My best friend is Noah, who is really cool.
I watch trains on TV,
Playing cars is lots of fun for me.
I just love sandwiches to eat,
And sometimes banana for a treat.
Black is a colour I like a lot,
My pirate is the best present I ever got.
My favourite person is Daddy, who is a gem,
So this, my first poem, is just for them!

Joshua Wheeler (4)
Little Rascals Nurseries, Tunbridge Wells

My First Poem

My name is Sophie and I go to preschool,
My best friend is Mummy, who is really cool.
I watch Frozen on TV,
Playing with toys is lots of fun for me.
I just love hot pot to eat,
And sometimes custard for a treat.
Pink is a colour I like a lot,
My doll is the best present I ever got.
My favourite person is Elsa, who is a gem,
So this, my first poem, is just for them!

Sophie Loftus (4)
Little Rascals Nurseries, Tunbridge Wells

My First Poem

My name is **Jaxon** and I go to preschool,
My best friend is **Mummy**, who is really cool.
I watch **Teenage Mutant Ninja Turtles** on TV,
Playing **with my action figures** is lots of fun for me.
I just love **sausages, beans, chips and pizza** to eat,
And sometimes **ice cream** for a treat.
Black and blue are colours I like a lot,
My **Ninja Turtle toys** are the best present I ever got.
My favourite people are **Mummy and Daddy**, who are gems,
So this, my first poem, is just for them!

Jaxon Duddy (4)
Pinewood Family Group Preschool, Farnborough

My First Poem

My name is Simbarashe and I go to preschool,
My best friend is Celine, who is really cool.
I watch Peppa Pig on TV,
Playing football is lots of fun for me.
I just love rice and ketchup to eat,
And sometimes ice cream for a treat.
Blue is a colour I like a lot,
My yellow truck is the best present I ever got.
My favourite person is Mummy, who is a gem,
So this, my first poem, is just for them!

Simbarashe Kayden Mapeta (4)
Pinewood Family Group Preschool, Farnborough

My First Poem

My name is Oscar and I go to preschool,
My best friend is Connor and Louie, who are really cool.
I watch Jake and the Neverland pirates on TV,
Playing games on my tablet and with my cars is lots of fun for me.
I just love pizza and pasta to eat,
And sometimes chocolate and ice cream for a treat.
Green is a colour I like a lot,
My remote-controlled car and Transformers are the best present I ever got.
My favourite person is my mummy, who is a gem,
So this, my first poem, is just for them!

Oscar Mason Eales (4)
Pinewood Family Group Preschool, Farnborough

My First Poem

My name is Alfee and I go to preschool,
My best friend is Sam, who is really cool.
I watch PAW Patrol on TV,
Playing with my cars is lots of fun for me.
I just love pasta and peas to eat,
And sometimes chocolate for a treat.
Green is a colour I like a lot,
My PAW Patrol toys are the best present
I ever got.
My favourite person is Mummy, who is a gem,
So this, my first poem, is just for them!

Alfee-Jai Sterriker-Dixon (2)
Pinewood Family Group Preschool, Farnborough

My First Poem

My name is **Rebecca** and I go to preschool,
My best friend is **Summer, my cousin**, who is really cool.
I watch **Frozen** on TV,
Playing **with dollies** is lots of fun for me.
I just love **bananas** to eat,
And sometimes **chocolate buttons** for a treat.
Pink is a colour I like a lot,
My **slide** is the best present I ever got.
My favourite person is **Nanny Kate**, who is a gem,
So this, my first poem, is just for them!

Rebecca Emily Stock (2)
Pinewood Family Group Preschool, Farnborough

My First Poem

My name is Emily and I go to preschool,
My best friend is Charlotte, who is really cool.
I watch Peppa Pig on TV,
Playing hide-and-seek is lots of fun for me.
I just love banana chips to eat,
And sometimes Kinder egg chocolate for a treat.
Green is a colour I like a lot,
My LeapPad Platinum is the best present
I ever got.
My favourite person is Mummy, who is a gem,
So this, my first poem, is just for them!

Emily Abbots (3)
Pinewood Family Group Preschool, Farnborough

My First Poem

My name is **Summer** and I go to preschool,
My best friend is **Autumn**, who is really cool.
I watch **Frozen, mermaids and ponies** on TV,
Playing with **Play-doh** is lots of fun for me.
I just love **fish fingers** to eat,
And sometimes **sweets** for a treat.
Purple and pink are colours I like a lot,
My **robot** is the best present I ever got.
My favourite person is **Father Christmas**, who is a gem,
So this, my first poem, is just for them!

Summer Facchini (2)
Pinewood Family Group Preschool, Farnborough

My First Poem

My name is Bruno and I go to preschool,
My best friend is Louie, who is really cool.
I watch a T-rex on TV,
Playing T-rexes is lots of fun for me.
I just love sweeties and strawberries to eat,
And sometimes choccie eggs for a treat.
Blue is a colour I like a lot,
My T-rex is the best present I ever got.
My favourite person is Daddy, who is a gem,
So this, my first poem, is just for them!

Bruno Alexander Ford (3)
Pinewood Family Group Preschool, Farnborough

My First Poem

My name is Sashwat and I go to preschool,
My best friend is Edif, who is really cool.
I watch Curious George, Power Rangers and Avengers Assemble on TV,
Playing with toys is lots of fun for me.
I just love apple to eat,
And sometimes juice for a treat.
Blue is a colour I like a lot,
My Batcave is the best present I ever got.
My favourite person is my mamu, who is a gem,
So this, my first poem, is just for them!

Sashwat Kiran Gurung (3)
Pinewood Family Group Preschool, Farnborough

My First Poem

My name is **Hazel** and I go to preschool,
My best friend is **Daniella**, who is really cool.
I watch **Big Cats** on TV,
Playing **catch** is lots of fun for me.
I just love **broccoli** to eat,
And sometimes **marshmallows toasted** for a treat.
Pink is a colour I like a lot,
My **bright pink horse** is the best present I ever got.
My favourite person is **William**, who is a gem,
So this, my first poem, is just for them!

Hazel Violet Booth (4)

Pinewood Family Group Preschool, Farnborough

My First Poem

My name is Amelia and I go to preschool,
My best friend is Louis, who is really cool.
I watch Milkshake on TV,
Playing with Bethany is lots of fun for me.
I just love carrots to eat,
And sometimes chocolate eggs for a treat.
Pink, purple and blue are colours I like a lot,
My Anna dress is the best present I ever got.
My favourite person is Mummy, who is a gem,
So this, my first poem, is just for them!

Amelia Cooles (3)
Pinewood Family Group Preschool, Farnborough

My First Poem

My name is **Astley** and I go to preschool,
My best friend is **Ruby**, who is really cool.
I watch **Bing** on TV,
Playing **with trains, cars and boats**
is lots of fun for me.
I just love **sausages and chips** to eat,
And sometimes **ice cream** for a treat.
Green is a colour I like a lot,
My **ride-on tractor** is the best present I ever got.
My favourite person is **my mum**, who is a gem,
So this, my first poem, is just for them!

Astley Povey (3)
Pinewood Family Group Preschool, Farnborough

My First Poem

My name is **Riley** and I go to preschool,

My best friend is **Elliott**, who is really cool.

I watch **Ninja Turtles** on TV,

Playing **with Imaginext toys** is lots of fun for me.

I just love **pasta and chips** to eat,

And sometimes **popcorn** for a treat.

Light blue is a colour I like a lot,

My **quadbike** is the best present I ever got.

My favourite person is **Daddy**, who is a gem,

So this, my first poem, is just for them!

Riley Willis (3)
Pinewood Family Group Preschool, Farnborough

My First Poem

My name is **Betty Rose Grice** and I go to preschool,
My best friend is **Isabelle**, who is really cool.
I watch **Topsy and Tim, Bob the Builder and Peppa Pig** on TV,
Playing **nurseries and mummies and daddies** is lots of fun for me.
I just love **yoghurt, granola, chips and baked beans** to eat,
And sometimes **chocolate** for a treat.
Red is a colour I like a lot,
My **orangutan puppet (Ugo)** is the best present I ever got.
My favourite person is **Winnie Mary-Joy, my sister**, who is a gem,
So this, my first poem, is just for them!

Betty Rose Grice (4)
Play Time Under 5s, Hove

My First Poem

My name is Isabelle and I go to preschool,
My best friend is Tilly, who is really cool.
I watch Toy Story on TV,
Playing with my toys is lots of fun for me.
I just love chips to eat,
And sometimes chocolate for a treat.
Purple and pink are colours I like a lot,
My Woody is the best present I ever got.
My favourite person is Tilly, who is a gem,
So this, my first poem, is just for them!

Isabelle Levett (4)
Puddleducks Day Nursery, Baldock

My First Poem

My name is **Nina** and I go to preschool,
My best friend is **Hallie**, who is really cool.
I watch **Fireman Sam** on TV,
Playing **hand painting** is lots of fun for me.
I just love **pasta** to eat,
And sometimes **chocolate** for a treat.
Pink is a colour I like a lot,
My **monkey blanket** is the best present I ever got.
My favourite person is **Daddy**, who is a gem,
So this, my first poem, is just for them!

Nina White (3)
Puddleducks Day Nursery, Baldock

My First Poem

My name is Alex and I go to preschool,
My best friend is Mummy, who is really cool.
I watch Smurfs on TV,
Playing with my helicopters is lots of fun for me.
I just love pasta to eat,
And sometimes stickers for a treat.
Yellow is a colour I like a lot,
My tablet is the best present I ever got.
My favourite person is Mummy, who is a gem,
So this, my first poem, is just for them!

Alex Picard-Cook (3)
Puddleducks Day Nursery, Baldock

My First Poem

My name is Oscar and I go to preschool,
My best friend is Cerys, who is really cool.
I watch Star Wars on TV,
Playing Woody and Buzz is lots of fun for me.
I just love macaroni and cheese to eat,
And sometimes a lolly from the tin for a treat.
Pink and purple are colours I like a lot,
My DVDs are the best present I ever got.
My favourite person is Mummy, who is a gem,
So this, my first poem, is just for them!

Oscar Lynam (4)
Puddleducks Day Nursery, Baldock

My First Poem

My name is **Aubrey** and I go to preschool,
My best friend is **Mummy**, who is really cool.
I watch **Peppa Pig** on TV,
Playing **with my new cars** is lots of fun for me.
I just love **pancakes** to eat,
And sometimes **more cars** for a treat.
Red is a colour I like a lot,
My **spinning things for my garage** is the best present I ever got.
My favourite person is **Daddy**, who is a gem,
So this, my first poem, is just for them!

Aubrey Murphy-Wearmouth (3)
Puddleducks Day Nursery, Baldock

My First Poem

My name is Cerys and I go to preschool,
My best friend is Amelia, who is really cool.
I watch Sleeping Beauty on TV,
Playing with Baby Born is lots of fun for me.
I just love bread to eat,
And sometimes chocolate biscuits for a treat.
Pink is a colour I like a lot,
My cupcake bicycle is the best present I ever got.
My favourite person is Amelia, who is a gem,
So this, my first poem, is just for them!

Cerys Evans (3)
Puddleducks Day Nursery, Baldock

My First Poem

My name is Oskar and I go to preschool,
My best friend is Jake, who is really cool.
I watch PAW Patrol on TV,
Playing with my dinosaur cards is lots of fun for me.
I just love malt loaf and scones to eat,
And sometimes chocolate for a treat.
Red and blue are colours I like a lot,
My daddy is the best present I ever got.
My favourite person is Daddy, who is a gem,
So this, my first poem, is just for them!

Oskar Francis (4)
Puddleducks Day Nursery, Baldock

My First Poem

My name is Amelia and I go to preschool,
My best friend is Cerys, who is really cool.
I watch CBeebies and Tiny Pop on TV,
Playing with my doll's house is lots of fun for me.
I just love pasta bake to eat,
And sometimes marshmallows for a treat.
Yellow, orange and pink are colours I like a lot,
My stories are the best present I ever got.
My favourite person is Mummy, who is a gem,
So this, my first poem, is just for them!

Amelia Ramirez-Baez (4)
Puddleducks Day Nursery, Baldock

My First Poem

My name is Frankie and I go to preschool,
My best friend is Mummy, who is really cool.
I watch Mr Tumble on TV,
Playing with cars is lots of fun for me.
I just love rice and mince to eat,
And sometimes an apple for a treat.
Green and blue are colours I like a lot,
My cars are the best presents I ever got.
My favourite person is Daddy, who is a gem,
So this, my first poem, is just for them!

Frankie Zwirner (3)
Puddleducks Day Nursery, Baldock

My First Poem

My name is Sofia and I go to preschool,
My best friend is Amelia, who is really cool.
I watch Harry Potter on TV,
Playing with my dolls is lots of fun for me.
I just love peas and sweetcorn to eat,
And sometimes sweets for a treat.
Pink is a colour I like a lot,
My Ginny doll is the best present I ever got.
My favourite people are Faye and Daddy, who are gems,
So this, my first poem, is just for them!

Sofia Jones (4)
Puddleducks Day Nursery, Baldock

My First Poem

My name is Maxwell and I go to preschool,
My best friend is Harry, who is really cool.
I watch Stick Man on TV,
Playing with cars is lots of fun for me.
I just love sausages to eat,
And sometimes chocolate for a treat.
Black is a colour I like a lot,
My cars are the best presents I ever got.
My favourite person is Daddy, who is a gem,
So this, my first poem, is just for them!

Maxwell Vinyard (3)
Puddleducks Day Nursery, Baldock

My First Poem

My name is **Iona** and I go to preschool,

My best friend is **Isabel**, who is really cool.

I watch **Peppa Pig** on TV,

Playing **with building blocks** is lots of fun for me.

I just love **mince pies** to eat,

And sometimes **biscuits** for a treat.

Red is a colour I like a lot,

My **teddy** is the best present I ever got.

My favourite people are **Mummy and Daddy**, who are gems,

So this, my first poem, is just for them!

Iona Thompson-Nisbet (4)
Puddleducks Day Nursery, Baldock

My First Poem

My name is Edward and I go to preschool,
My best friend is Miles, who is really cool.
I watch Peppa Pig on TV,
Playing with fire engines is lots of fun for me.
I just love sausages to eat,
And sometimes chocolate for a treat.
Yellow is a colour I like a lot,
My red present is the best present I ever got.
My favourite person is Daddy, who is a gem,
So this, my first poem, is just for them!

Edward Rofe (3)
Puddleducks Day Nursery, Baldock

My First Poem

My name is Samuel and I go to preschool,
My best friend is Mummy, who is really cool.
I watch Peppa Pig on TV,
Playing with my dumper truck is lots of fun for me.
I just love pie to eat,
And sometimes stars and playing with Lego for a treat.
Yellow and green are colours I like a lot,
My dumper truck is the best present I ever got.
My favourite person is Daddy, who is a gem,
So this, my first poem, is just for them!

Samuel Evans (3)
Puddleducks Day Nursery, Baldock

My First Poem

My name is **Keira** and I go to preschool,
My best friend is **Samuel**, who is really cool.
I watch **PAW Patrol** on TV,
Playing **with toys** is lots of fun for me.
I just love **sandwiches** to eat,
And sometimes **sweeties** for a treat.
Pink, blue, red and orange are colours I like a lot,
My **Poppy** is the best present I ever got.
My favourite people are **Mummy, Daddy and my brother**, who are gems,
So this, my first poem, is just for them!

Keira Parkinson (3)

Puddleducks Day Nursery, Baldock

My First Poem

My name is Zoe and I go to preschool,
My best friend is Dexta, who is really cool.
I watch CBeebies on TV,
Playing Connect 4 is lots of fun for me.
I just love ham sandwiches to eat,
And sometimes playing with toys for a treat.
Yellow is a colour I like a lot,
My Furchester Hotel is the best present I ever got.
My favourite person is Dexta, who is a gem,
So this, my first poem, is just for them!

Zoe Wood (4)
Puddleducks Day Nursery, Baldock

My First Poem

My name is **Aoife** and I go to preschool,
My best friend is **Plum**, who is really cool.
I watch **Frozen** on TV,
Playing **in the dark** is lots of fun for me.
I just love **peas** to eat,
And sometimes **an egg** for a treat.
Blue is a colour I like a lot,
My **bike** is the best present I ever got.
My favourite person is **Daddy**, who is a gem,
So this, my first poem, is just for them!

Aoife Doherty (3)
Puddleducks Day Nursery, Baldock

My First Poem

My name is Jessica and I go to preschool,
My best friend is Maddie, who is really cool.
I watch Little Red Riding Hood on TV,
Playing with my doll doll is lots of fun for me.
I just love broccoli to eat,
And sometimes Smarties for a treat.
Purple is a colour I like a lot,
My doll doll is the best present I ever got.
My favourite person is Annabel, who is a gem,
So this, my first poem, is just for them!

Jessica Green (3)
Puddleducks Day Nursery, Baldock

My First Poem

My name is Bethany and I go to preschool,
My best friend is Sophie, who is really cool.
I watch Frozen on TV,
Playing with 'Let It Go' toys is lots of fun for me.
I just love crackers to eat,
And sometimes chocolate for a treat.
Pink is a colour I like a lot,
My chocolate is the best present I ever got.
My favourite person is Sophie, who is a gem,
So this, my first poem, is just for them!

Bethany Hemmings (3)
Puddleducks Day Nursery, Baldock

My First Poem

My name is **Noah** and I go to preschool,
My best friend is **Seth**, who is really cool.
I watch **Ben & Holly** on TV,
Playing **with my dinosaurs** is lots of fun for me.
I just love **lasagne** to eat,
And sometimes **sweets** for a treat.
Green, red and blue are colours I like a lot,
My **tool bench** is the best present I ever got.
My favourite person is **Seth**, who is a gem,
So this, my first poem, is just for them!

Noah Fitzgerald (3)
Puddleducks Day Nursery, Baldock

My First Poem

My name is **Benjamin** and I go to preschool,
My best friend is **Daddy**, who is really cool.
I watch **CBeebies** on TV,
Playing **with cars** is lots of fun for me.
I just love **pasta** to eat,
And sometimes **crisps** for a treat.
Pink is a colour I like a lot,
My **bus** is the best present I ever got.
My favourite person is **Daddy**, who is a gem,
So this, my first poem, is just for them!

Benjamin Cape (3)
Puddleducks Day Nursery, Baldock

My First Poem

My name is **Mason** and I go to preschool,
My best friend is **Oskar**, who is really cool.
I watch **Wallykazam!** on TV,
Playing **diggers** is lots of fun for me.
I just love **crunchy nut** to eat,
And sometimes **sweeties, toys and chocolate** for a treat.
Pink is a colour I like a lot,
My **toy crane** is the best present I ever got.
My favourite person is **my mummy**, who is a gem,
So this, my first poem, is just for them!

Mason Hunt (3)
Puddleducks Day Nursery, Baldock

My First Poem

My name is **Stefan** and I go to preschool,
My best friend is **Mummy**, who is really cool.
I watch **PAW Patrol** on TV,
Playing **fire engines** is lots of fun for me.
I just love **strawberries, bananas and grapes** to eat,
And sometimes **sweets and Smarties** for a treat.
Red and green are colours I like a lot,
My **new bike and new car** are the best presents I ever got.
My favourite people are **Mummy and Daddy**, who are gems,
So this, my first poem, is just for them!

Stefan Centala (3)
Puddleducks Day Nursery, Baldock

My First Poem

My name is **Luca** and I go to preschool,
My best friends are **Ben and Harry**, who are really cool.
I watch **Peter Rabbit** on TV,
Playing **Thomas** is lots of fun for me.
I just love **pasta** to eat,
And sometimes **a Kinder egg** for a treat.
Blue is a colour I like a lot,
My **white car** is the best present I ever got.
My favourite person is **Daddy**, who is a gem,
So this, my first poem, is just for them!

Luca Casalini (3)
Puddleducks Day Nursery, Baldock

My First Poem

My name is Erin and I go to preschool,
My best friend is Olivia, who is really cool.
I watch Scooby-Doo and PAW Patrol on TV,
Playing with flowers and Play-Doh are lots of fun for me.
I just love chickeny rice to eat,
And sometimes strawberries for a treat.
Blue is a colour I like a lot,
My PAW Patrols are the best presents I ever got.
My favourite person is mummy, who is a gem,
So this, my first poem, is just for them!

Erin Holly Robinson (3)
Puddleducks Day Nursery, Baldock

My First Poem

My name is Summer and I go to preschool,
My best friend is Alex, who is really cool.
I watch Mia and Tinkerbell on TV,
Playing Rapunzel is lots of fun for me.
I just love spaghetti Bolognese to eat,
And sometimes chocolate for a treat.
Pink and purple are colours I like a lot,
My Jessie and Bullseye are the best presents I ever got.
My favourite people are Mummy and Daddy, who are gems,
So this, my first poem, is just for them!

Summer Haer (3)
Puddleducks Day Nursery, Baldock

My First Poem

My name is **Zavier** and I go to preschool,
My best friends are **Oscar and Jake**, who are really cool.
I watch **Power Rangers** on TV,
Playing **Power Rangers** is lots of fun for me.
I just love **toast** to eat,
And sometimes **a toy** for a treat.
Red is a colour I like a lot,
My **Mega Force robot** is the best present I ever got.
My favourite person is **Mummy**, who is a gem,
So this, my first poem, is just for them!

Zavier Lemaitre (4)
Puddleducks Day Nursery, Baldock

My First Poem

My name is Cadi and I go to preschool,
My best friend is Summer, who is really cool.
I watch Peppa Pig and Nelly the Elephant on TV,
Playing music is lots of fun for me.
I just love sandwiches to eat,
And sometimes chocolate coins for a treat.
Pink is a colour I like a lot,
My dinosaur is the best present I ever got.
My favourite people are Mummy and Daddy,
who are gems,
So this, my first poem, is just for them!

Cadi Hâf Bradford (3)
Puddleducks Day Nursery, Baldock

My First Poem

My name is Isabel and I go to preschool,
My best friend is Skye, who is really cool.
I watch Barbie Fairy on TV,
Playing dominoes is lots of fun for me.
I just love sausages to eat,
And sometimes chocolate for a treat.
Pink is a colour I like a lot,
My dolls are the best present I ever got.
My favourite person is everybody, who are gems,
So this, my first poem, is just for them!

Isabel Gale (4)
Puddleducks Day Nursery, Baldock

My First Poem

My name is **Matthew** and I go to preschool,
My best friend is **Maxwell**, who is really cool.
I watch **Topsy and Tim** on TV,
Playing **and building** is lots of fun for me.
I just love **pasta** to eat,
And sometimes **sweets** for a treat.
Pink is a colour I like a lot,
My **Fireman Sam** is the best present I ever got.
My favourite person is **Mummy**, who is a gem,
So this, my first poem, is just for them!

Matthew Pike (3)
Puddleducks Day Nursery, Baldock

My First Poem

My name is Jacob and I go to preschool,
My best friend is Connor, who is really cool.
I watch Scooby-Doo on TV,
Playing with Lego is lots of fun for me.
I just love fish cakes and chips to eat,
And sometimes McDonald's for a treat.
Red is a colour I like a lot,
My Scooby-Doo is the best present I ever got.
My favourite people are Mummy and Daddy,
who are gems,
So this, my first poem, is just for them!

Jacob Adam King (4)
Puddleducks Day Nursery, Baldock

My First Poem

My name is Zoe and I go to preschool,
My best friends are Amelie and Amelia, who are really cool.
I watch Frozen on TV,
Playing Peppa Pig is lots of fun for me.
I just love spaghetti Bolognese to eat,
And sometimes ice cream for a treat.
Red and green are colours I like a lot,
My Flopsy is the best present I ever got.
My favourite people are Mummy and Daddy, who are gems,
So this, my first poem, is just for them!

Zoe Barr (4)
Puddleducks Day Nursery, Baldock

My First Poem

My name is William and I go to preschool,
My best friend is Olivia, who is really cool.
I watch Peppa Pig on TV,
Playing with cars is lots of fun for me.
I just love ham and peas to eat,
And sometimes sweeties for a treat.
Pink and blue are colours I like a lot,
My swimming lessons are the best present I ever got.
My favourite people are Mummy, Daddy and Rhys, who are gems,
So this, my first poem, is just for them!

William Ioan Davies (3)
Puddleducks Day Nursery, Baldock

My First Poem

My name is **Brandon** and I go to preschool,
My best friend is **Dexter**, who is really cool.
I watch **Star Wars** on TV,
Playing **Star Wars** is lots of fun for me.
I just love **sausages and pancakes** to eat,
And sometimes **lollipops** for a treat.
Purple is a colour I like a lot,
My **big dusty** is the best present I ever got.
My favourite person is **Daddy**, who is a gem,
So this, my first poem, is just for them!

Brandon Delaney (3)
Puddleducks Day Nursery, Baldock

My First Poem

My name is Max and I go to preschool,
My best friend is Daniel, who is really cool.
I watch PAW Patrol on TV,
Playing the trumpet is lots of fun for me.
I just love pasta to eat,
And sometimes sweeties for a treat.
Blue is a colour I like a lot,
My pens are the best present I ever got.
My favourite person is Daniel, who is a gem,
So this, my first poem, is just for them!

Max Middleton (3)
Puddleducks Day Nursery, Baldock

My First Poem

My name is **Finlay** and I go to preschool,
My best friends are **my mummy and daddy**, who are really cool.
I watch **PAW Patrol** on TV,
Playing **with trains** is lots of fun for me.
I just love **spaghetti hoops** to eat,
And sometimes **chocolate stars** for a treat.
Red is a colour I like a lot,
My **toys** are the best present I ever got.
My favourite person is **Harry**, who is a gem,
So this, my first poem, is just for them!

Finlay Leach (3)
Red Fox Day Nursery, Marlow

My First Poem

My name is Harry and I go to preschool,
My best friend is Summer, who is really cool.
I watch Blaze, PAW Patrol, Peppa Pig and Thomas on TV,
Playing on my iPad is lots of fun for me.
I just love curry to eat,
And sometimes a lollipop for a treat.
Green is a colour I like a lot,
My PAW Patrols are the best present I ever got.
My favourite person is Daddy, who is a gem,
So this, my first poem, is just for them!

Harry Shillito (3)
Red Fox Day Nursery, Marlow

My First Poem

My name is Jess and I go to preschool,
My best friend is Darcie, who is really cool.
I watch Paw Patrol on TV,
Playing with Darcie is lots of fun for me.
I just love pears to eat,
And sometimes a lollipop for a treat.
Pink is a colour I like a lot,
My princess dress is the best present I ever got.
My favourite person is Daddy, who is a gem,
So this, my first poem, is just for them!

Jess Rooney (3)
Red Fox Day Nursery, Marlow

My First Poem

My name is Cooper and I go to preschool,
My best friend is George, who is really cool.
I watch ninjas on TV,
Playing with my Thomas train is lots of fun for me.
I just love a roast dinner to eat,
And sometimes chocolate ice cream for a treat.
Pink is a colour I like a lot,
My Thomas toothbrush is the best present I ever got.
My favourite people are Mummy, Daddy, Kira and Murray, who are gems,
So this, my first poem, is just for them!

Cooper Burstow (3)
St Gabriel's Playgroup, Billingshurst

My First Poem

My name is George and I go to preschool,
My best friend is Jayden, who is really cool.
I watch Peppa Pig on TV,
Playing with my camera is lots of fun for me.
I just love pizza to eat,
And sometimes go to the sweetie shop for a treat.
Blue is a colour I like a lot,
My Dragon Thomas Drop is the best present I ever got.
My favourite people are Mummy, Daddy and my brother James, who are gems,
So this, my first poem, is just for them!

George Evans (4)
St Gabriel's Playgroup, Billingshurst

My First Poem

My name is Isabelle and I go to preschool,
My best friend is Evlyn, who is really cool.
I watch Peppa Pig on TV,
Playing with my dolls is lots of fun for me.
I just love spaghetti Bolognese and fish fingers to eat,
And sometimes a Mini Egg yoghurt for a treat.
Purple and pink are colours I like a lot,
My Rapunzel dress is the best present I ever got.
My favourite people are Daddy, Mummy and all my friends, who are gems,
So this, my first poem, is just for them!

Isabelle Carter (3)
St Gabriel's Playgroup, Billingshurst

My First Poem

My name is Maddie and I go to preschool,
My best friend is Lily Mae, who is really cool.
I watch Blaze and the Monster Machines on TV,
Playing with my Elsa and Anna dolls is lots of fun for me.
I just love a roast dinner to eat,
And sometimes lollipops for a treat.
Pink is a colour I like a lot,
My Ninja Turtle teddies are the best present I ever got.
My favourite people are Mummy, Daddy and Robyn, my big sister, who are gems,
So this, my first poem, is just for them!

Maddie Twaddle (4)
St Gabriel's Playgroup, Billingshurst

My First Poem

My name is Chloe and I go to preschool,
My best friend is Laura, who is really cool.
I watch Fireman Sam on TV,
Playing on the bikes is lots of fun for me.
I just love pizza to eat,
And sometimes have chocolate for a treat.
Green is a colour I like a lot,
My bike is the best present I ever got.
My favourite people are Katie and Mummy,
who are gems,
So this, my first poem, is just for them!

Chloe Tillotson (4)
St Gabriel's Playgroup, Billingshurst

My First Poem

My name is Raphael and I go to preschool,
My best friend is Laura, who is really cool.
I watch Mr Bean on TV,
Playing with Postman Pat toys is lots of fun for me.
I just love egg on toast to eat,
And sometimes a Kinder egg for a treat.
Red is a colour I like a lot,
My Postman Pat toys are the best presents I ever got.
My favourite person is Twinkle the cat, who is a gem,
So this, my first poem, is just for them!

Raphael White (3)
St Gabriel's Playgroup, Billingshurst

My First Poem

My name is Jayden and I go to preschool,
My best friend is George, who is really cool.
I watch PAW Patrol and Batman on TV,
Playing on my dinosaur bike is lots of fun for me.
I just love pasta and cheesy chips to eat,
And sometimes chocolate for a treat.
Green is a colour I like a lot,
My PAW Patrol squirty bath toys are the best present I ever got.
My favourite people are Mummy and all my family, who are gems,
So this, my first poem, is just for them!

Jayden James Foster-Hopkins (4)
St Gabriel's Playgroup, Billingshurst

My First Poem

My name is Brooke and I go to preschool,
My best friend is everyone, who are really cool.
I watch Panda Moon on TV,
Playing with my Frozen jigsaw is lots of fun for me.
I just love chicken and rice to eat,
And sometimes yoghurt for a treat.
Pink is a colour I like a lot,
My Frozen Elsa doll is the best present I ever got.
My favourite people are Mummy, Daddy, Daisy and Sophia, who are gems,
So this, my first poem, is just for them!

Brooke Hyde (4)
St Gabriel's Playgroup, Billingshurst

My First Poem

My name is Rosie and I go to preschool,
My best friend is Ellie, who is really cool.
I watch My Little Pony on TV,
Playing ponies is lots of fun for me.
I just love pizza to eat,
And sometimes Smiley Faces for a treat.
Red and purple are colours I like a lot,
My crocodile is the best present I ever got.
My favourite person is Aidan, who is a gem,
So this, my first poem, is just for them!

Rosie Faith Bryan (4)
St John's Playgroup, Harrogate

My First Poem

My name is Freya and I go to preschool,
My best friend is Ellie, who is really cool.
I watch Elsa and Anna on TV,
Playing Pop-Up Pirates is lots of fun for me.
I just love chocolate to eat,
And sometimes sweeties for a treat.
Pink is a colour I like a lot,
My Elsa and Anna dolls are the best presents
I ever got.
My favourite person is Lucy, who is a gem,
So this, my first poem, is just for them!

Freya Manley (4)
St John's Playgroup, Harrogate

My First Poem

My name is Charlie and I go to preschool,
My best friend is Dillan, who is really cool.
I watch Horrid Henry on TV,
Playing with my train track is lots of fun for me.
I just love lasagne to eat,
And sometimes Bear Paws for a treat.
Red is a colour I like a lot,
My bumpy train track is the best present I ever got.
My favourite person is Daddy, who is a gem,
So this, my first poem, is just for them!

Charlie Wilson
St John's Playgroup, Harrogate

My First Poem

My name is Dillan and I go to preschool,
My best friend is Charlie, who is really cool.
I watch PAW Patrol on TV,
Playing monsters is lots of fun for me.
I just love pizza to eat,
And sometimes a fruit roll for a treat.
Blue and red are colours I like a lot,
My crossing for my train track is the best present I ever got.
My favourite person is Charlie, who is a gem,
So this, my first poem, is just for them!

Dillan Foster (3)
St John's Playgroup, Harrogate

My First Poem

My name is Daniel and I go to preschool,
My best friend is Harvey, who is really cool.
I watch LazyTown on TV,
Playing with my lightsaber is lots of fun for me.
I just love grapes and bananas to eat,
And sometimes a sausage roll for a treat.
Green is a colour I like a lot,
My silver lightsaber is the best present I ever got.
My favourite person is Aidan, who is a gem,
So this, my first poem, is just for them!

Daniel Hewson (4)
St John's Playgroup, Harrogate

My First Poem

My name is **Hazel** and I go to preschool,
My best friend is **K-K**, who is really cool.
I watch **PAW Patrol, Peppa Pig and 101 Dalmatians** on TV,
Playing **Mario** is lots of fun for me.
I just love **sweeties** to eat,
And sometimes **sweeties (again)** for a treat.
Red is a colour I like a lot,
My **hamsters** are the best present I ever got.
My favourite person is **K-K**, who is a gem,
So this, my first poem, is just for them!

Hazel Alison Thurley (3)
St John's Playgroup, Harrogate

My First Poem

My name is Lucy and I go to preschool,
My best friend is Kayleigh, who is really cool.
I watch Dora and Friends on TV,
Playing mums and dads is lots of fun for me.
I just love apples, strawberries and grapes to eat,
And sometimes chocolate for a treat.
Pink is a colour I like a lot,
My Elsa doll is the best present I ever got.
My favourite person is Freya, who is a gem,
So this, my first poem, is just for them!

Lucy Nicholls (4)
St John's Playgroup, Harrogate

My First Poem

My name is **K-K** and I go to preschool,
My best friend is **Hazel**, who is really cool.
I watch **Blaze and PAW Patrol** on TV,
Playing **with my Frozen dollies** is lots of fun for me.
I just love **chocolate porridge** to eat,
And sometimes **marmalade on toast** for a treat.
Pink, yellow, red, blue and purple are colours I like a lot,
My **hamster, Fluffy** is the best present I ever got.
My favourite person is **Liam**, who is a gem,
So this, my first poem, is just for them!

Kayleigh Louise Carney (4)
St John's Playgroup, Harrogate

My First Poem

My name is **Nathan** and I go to preschool,
My best friend is **Harrison**, who is really cool.
I watch **Adventure Time** on TV,
Playing **with a car that is really cool** is lots of fun for me.
I just love **potatoes and bananas** to eat,
And sometimes **jelly** for a treat.
Gold is a colour I like a lot,
My **walking robot** is the best present I ever got.
My favourite person is **Mummy**, who is a gem,
So this, my first poem, is just for them!

Nathan Rickman (4)
Starfish Day Nursery, Fareham

My First Poem

My name is **Isabelle** and I go to preschool,
My best friends are **Amelia and Kayleigh**, who are really cool.
I watch **Peppa Pig and PAW Patrol** on TV,
Playing **with dinosaurs** is lots of fun for me.
I just love **grapes, strawberries and apples** to eat,
And sometimes **crisps** for a treat.
Pink is a colour I like a lot,
My **Frozen bicycle** is the best present I ever got.
My favourite person is **Mama**, who is a gem,
So this, my first poem, is just for them!

Isabelle Rose Cox (3)
Starfish Day Nursery, Fareham

My First Poem

My name is Caleb and I go to preschool,
My best friend is John, who is really cool.
I watch Lightning McQueen on TV,
Playing games is lots of fun for me.
I just love peas to eat,
And sometimes sweeties for a treat.
Blue is a colour I like a lot,
My Minion sleeping bag is the best present
I ever got.
My favourite person is Mama, who is a gem,
So this, my first poem, is just for them!

Caleb Allen (3)
Starfish Day Nursery, Fareham

My First Poem

My name is Chloe, although Mum calls me Princess, and I go to preschool,
My best friend is a little boy from preschool, Peter, who is really cool.
I watch Care Bears and other girlie cartoons on TV,
Playing with Play-Doh and my Barbie with my mummy is lots of fun for me.
I just love tomatoes, mozzarella and my favourite, sweetcorn, to eat,
And sometimes my bear crisps or sweets for a treat.
Purple is the colour I love the most, but pink is a colour I like a lot,
My Barbie doll's house and my bunny is the best present I ever got.
My favourite people are my mummy, but also Daddy, who are gems,
So this, my first poem, is just for them!

Chloé Dos Santos (3)
Starlings Preschool, Basingstoke

My First Poem

My name is Owen and I go to preschool,
My best friends are Reuben and William who are really cool.
I watch Peter Rabbit on TV,
Playing Transformers is lots of fun for me.
I just love chips to eat,
And sometimes chocolate for a treat.
Pink is a colour I like a lot,
My monster truck is the best present I ever got.
My favourite person is Grandad, who is a gem,
So this, my first poem, is just for them!

Owen Stephen Leaney (3)
Starlings Preschool, Basingstoke

My First Poem

My name is Logan and I go to preschool,
My best friend is Isaac, who is really cool.
I watch Curious George and PAW Patrol on TV,
Playing with Play-Doh is lots of fun for me.
I just love burgers to eat,
And sometimes strawberries for a treat.
Green is a colour I like a lot,
My dinosaur is the best present I ever got.
My favourite person is Grandad, who is a gem,
So this, my first poem, is just for them!

Logan Billington (4)
Starlings Preschool, Basingstoke

My First Poem

My name is Emilia, but people call me Millie, and
I go to preschool,
My best friend is Bella-Rose, who is really cool.
I watch My Little Pony on TV,
Playing with my ponies is lots of fun for me.
I just love sausage and chips to eat,
And sometimes McDonald's for a treat.
Pink is a colour I like a lot,
My My Little Pony is the best present I ever got.
My favourite person is Mummy, who is a gem,
So this, my first poem, is just for them!

Emilia Wilkinson (2)
Starlings Preschool, Basingstoke

My First Poem

My name is **Marcus** and I go to preschool,
My best friend is **Jacob**, who is really cool.
I watch **Sofia the First** on TV,
Playing **with cars** is lots of fun for me.
I just love **strawberries** to eat,
And sometimes **a biscuit** for a treat.
Blue is a colour I like a lot,
My **pirate ship** is the best present I ever got.
My favourite person is **Mummy**, who is a gem,
So this, my first poem, is just for them!

Marcus Goddard (2)
Starlings Preschool, Basingstoke

My First Poem

My name is **Isla** and I go to preschool,
My best friends are **Ruby**, **Evie** and **India**, who are really cool.
I watch **Peppa Pig** on TV,
Playing **Blaze and the Monster Machines** is lots of fun for me.
I just love **cheese sandwiches and cheese** to eat,
And sometimes **chocolate cake** for a treat.
Red and blue are colours I like a lot,
My **Robofish** is the best present I ever got.
My favourite person is **Rhi**, who is a gem,
So this, my first poem, is just for them!

Isla Grace Amos (3)
Starlings Preschool, Basingstoke

My First Poem

My name is Evie and I go to preschool,
My best friend is Ruby, who is really cool.
I watch Peppa Pig on TV,
Playing with Doc McStuffins is lots of fun for me.
I just love oranges to eat,
And sometimes chocolate for a treat.
Pink is a colour I like a lot,
My pretty dress is the best present I ever got.
My favourite people are Ruby and Mummy, who are gems,
So this, my first poem, is just for them!

Evie Vickery (3)
Starlings Preschool, Basingstoke

My First Poem

My name is **Kaci** and I go to preschool,
My best friend is **Chloe**, who is really cool.
I watch **Dora** on TV,
Playing **babies** is lots of fun for me.
I just love **ham and sweets** to eat,
And sometimes **marshmallows** for a treat.
Purple is a colour I like a lot,
My **Peppa Pig bike** is the best present I ever got.
My favourite person is **Jamie**, who is a gem,
So this, my first poem, is just for them!

Kaci Thomas-Graham (3)
Starlings Preschool, Basingstoke

My First Poem

My name is **Evie-Mae** and I go to preschool,
My best friend is **Zac**, who is really cool.
I watch **Nemo** on TV,
Playing **with Play-Doh** is lots of fun for me.
I just love **pasta** to eat,
And sometimes **chocolate** for a treat.
Pink is a colour I like a lot,
My **Elsa** is the best present I ever got.
My favourite person is **Mummy**, who is a gem,
So this, my first poem, is just for them!

Evie-Mae Field (3)
Starlings Preschool, Basingstoke

My First Poem

My name is **Michael** and I go to preschool,
My best friend is **Xander**, who is really cool.
I watch **Mickey Mouse** on TV,
Playing **shooting with Nerf games** is lots of fun for me.
I just love **yoghurt with chocolate balls** to eat,
And sometimes **cake** for a treat.
Black is a colour I like a lot,
My **awesome car** is the best present I ever got.
My favourite person is **Daddy**, who is a gem,
So this, my first poem, is just for them!

Michael Waring (4)
Starlings Preschool, Basingstoke

My First Poem

My name is Callum and I go to preschool,
My best friends are Harry, Evie and Leighton, who are really cool.
I watch Team Umizoomi, Jake and the Neverland Pirates, and Blaze and the Monster Machines on TV,
Playing on my DS and with friends is lots of fun for me.
I just love pepperoni pizza and chicken nuggets and chips to eat,
And sometimes lollipops, cheese, grapes and biscuits for a treat.
Red is a colour I like a lot,
My lightsaber is the best present I ever got.
My favourite people are Mummy, Daddy and Harry, who are gems,
So this, my first poem, is just for them!

Callum Riley Embleton (4)
Starlings Preschool, Basingstoke

My First Poem

My name is Harrison and I go to preschool,
My best friend is Lennon, who is really cool.
I watch lots of movies on TV,
Playing with toys is lots of fun for me.
I just love chocolate bread to eat,
And sometimes biscuits for a treat.
Blue is a colour I like a lot,
My Thomas is the best present I ever got.
My favourite person is the Fat Controller, who is a gem,
So this, my first poem, is just for them!

Harrison Lee Brian Ford (3)
Starlings Preschool, Basingstoke

My First Poem

My name is Medeea and I go to preschool,
My best friend is Chloe, who is really cool.
I watch My Little Pony on TV,
Playing with toys is lots of fun for me.
I just love pasta with cheese to eat,
And sometimes milk for a treat.
Pink is a colour I like a lot,
My Peppa Pig house is the best present I ever got.
My favourite people are Daddy and Mum, who are gems,
So this, my first poem, is just for them!

Medeea Ana-Maria Biro (3)
Starlings Preschool, Basingstoke

My First Poem

My name is **Frankie** and I go to preschool,
My best friend is **Toby**, who is really cool.
I watch **Lightning McQueen** on TV,
Playing **with sand, Play-Doh and cars** is lots of fun for me.
I just love **hot dogs** to eat,
And sometimes **Kinder eggs** for a treat.
Blue, grey, brown and red are colours I like a lot,
My **Batman car** is the best present I ever got.
My favourite people are **Santa and Toby**, who are gems,
So this, my first poem, is just for them!

Frankie Gordon Potter (3)
Starlings Preschool, Basingstoke

My First Poem

My name is Olivia and I go to preschool,
My best friend is Maya, who is really cool.
I watch Frozen on TV,
Playing Barbies is lots of fun for me.
I just love prawn crackers to eat,
And sometimes lollies for a treat.
Red is a colour I like a lot,
My tablet is the best present I ever got.
My favourite person is Yasmin, who is a gem,
So this, my first poem, is just for them!

Olivia Rogers (4)
Starlings Preschool, Basingstoke

My First Poem

My name is Tytus and I go to preschool,
My best friend is Franek, who is really cool.
I watch Dora the Explorer on TV,
Playing with Play-Doh is lots of fun for me.
I just love pepperoni pizza to eat,
And sometimes sweets for a treat.
Pink is a colour I like a lot,
My magic wand is the best present I ever got.
My favourite people are my mum and dad, who are gems,
So this, my first poem, is just for them!

Tytus Mrozowski (4)
Starlings Preschool, Basingstoke

My First Poem

My name is **Keilan** and I go to preschool,
My best friend is **Hollie**, who is really cool.
I watch **Tom and Jerry** on TV,
Playing **with the track** is lots of fun for me.
I just love **pasta** to eat,
And sometimes **bourbons** for a treat.
Red is a colour I like a lot,
My **motor car** is the best present I ever got.
My favourite person is **Nanny**, who is a gem,
So this, my first poem, is just for them!

Keilan Farmer (3)
Starlings Preschool, Basingstoke

My First Poem

My name is Ella and I go to preschool,
My best friend is Jack, who is really cool.
I watch Peppa Pig on TV,
Playing with Play-doh is lots of fun for me.
I just love grapes and spaghetti to eat,
And sometimes chocolate buttons for a treat.
Orange and blue are colours I like a lot,
My Suzie Sheep is the best present I ever got.
My favourite person is Mummy, who is a gem,
So this, my first poem, is just for them!

Ella Robertson (3)
Starlings Preschool, Basingstoke

My First Poem

My name is Jalika and I go to preschool,
My best friend is Olivia, who is really cool.
I watch Ben & Holly on TV,
Playing dollies is lots of fun for me.
I just love smoked salmon and scrambled eggs to eat,
And sometimes biscuits for a treat.
Purple is a colour I like a lot,
My remote-controlled car is the best present I ever got.
My favourite person is my cousin Daisy, who is a gem,
So this, my first poem, is just for them!

Jalika Lehannah Camara (3)
Starlings Preschool, Basingstoke

My First Poem

My name is Al-Mahdi and I go to preschool,

My best friend is Taylor, who is really cool.

I watch Minions on TV,

Playing Spider-Man is lots of fun for me.

I just love veggies to eat,

And sometimes a Kinder Surprise egg for a treat.

Blue is a colour I like a lot,

My Spider-Man is the best present I ever got.

My favourite person is Mummy, who is a gem,

So this, my first poem, is just for them!

Al-Mahdi Uddin (4)
Starlings Preschool, Basingstoke

My First Poem

My name is Siddhartha and I go to preschool,
My best friend is Bailey, who is really cool.
I watch Lightning McQueen on TV,
Playing with Lightning McQueen and cars is lots of fun for me.
I just love grapes to eat,
And sometimes chocolate for a treat.
Red is a colour I like a lot,
My Baba (Father) is the best present I ever got.
My favourite person is Mummy, who is a gem,
So this, my first poem, is just for them!

Siddhartha Gurung (3)
Starlings Preschool, Basingstoke

My First Poem

My name is Toby and I go to preschool,

My best friend is Frankie, who is really cool.

I watch Cars on TV,

Playing Lightning McQueen is lots of fun for me.

I just love chips to eat,

And sometimes crisps for a treat.

Blue is a colour I like a lot,

My Lightning McQueen is the best present I ever got.

My favourite person is Sammy, who is a gem,

So this, my first poem, is just for them!

Toby Cowie (3)
Starlings Preschool, Basingstoke

My First Poem

My name is **Nathan** and I go to preschool,
My best friend is **Jack**, who is really cool.
I watch **Tom and Jerry, Teenage Turtles and Angry Birds** on TV,
Playing **dress-up with my Avenger costumes** is lots of fun for me.
I just love **grapes, apples, peaches and pizza** to eat,
And sometimes **chocolate buttons** for a treat.
Red is a colour I like a lot,
My **kids' Fire Tablet** is the best present I ever got.
My favourite person is **Marcus, my brother**, who is a gem,
So this, my first poem, is just for them!

Nathan Jones (3)
Starlings Preschool, Basingstoke

My First Poem

My name is Zac and I go to preschool,
My best friend is Evie-Mae, who is really cool.
I watch Miles From Tomorrow on TV,
Playing with my castle is lots of fun for me.
I just love spaghetti to eat,
And sometimes a pancake for a treat.
Blue is a colour I like a lot,
My Peppa Pig books are the best present I ever got.
My favourite person is Mummy, who is a gem,
So this, my first poem, is just for them!

Zac Roberts (3)
Starlings Preschool, Basingstoke

My First Poem

My name is Ethan and I go to preschool,
My best friend is Leyton, who is really cool.
I watch SpongeBob on TV,
Playing Star Wars is lots of fun for me.
I just love pizza to eat,
And sometimes sweets for a treat.
Blue is a colour I like a lot,
My Spider-Man car is the best present I ever got.
My favourite person is Dad, who is a gem,
So this, my first poem, is just for them!

Ethan Smith (4)
Starlings Preschool, Basingstoke

My First Poem

My name is Jimmy and I go to preschool,
My best friend is Emily, who is really cool.
I watch Hotel Transylvania on TV,
Playing dinosaurs is lots of fun for me.
I just love Marmite on toast to eat,
And sometimes blueberries for a treat.
Orange is a colour I like a lot,
My Woody costume is the best present I ever got.
My favourite person is Sophie, who is a gem,
So this, my first poem, is just for them!

Jimmy Say (2)
Starlings Preschool, Basingstoke

My First Poem

My name is **Max** and I go to preschool,
My best friends are **Myles and Evie**, who are really cool.
I watch **Peppa Pig** on TV,
Playing **Lego Jurassic Park on the Wii** is lots of fun for me.
I just love **honey** to eat,
And sometimes **chocolate honey** for a treat.
Yellow is a colour I like a lot,
My **car** is the best present I ever got.
My favourite people are **Mummy and Daddy**, who are gems,
So this, my first poem, is just for them!

Max Barrett (4)
Therfield Village Preschool, Royston

My First Poem

My name is Charley and I go to preschool,
My best friend is James, who is really cool.
I watch Thomas on TV,
Playing with Thomas and Percy is lots of
fun for me.
I just love pasta to eat,
And sometimes cake for a treat.
Green is a colour I like a lot,
My Thomas Tank Engine is the best present
I ever got.
My favourite person is Amelie, who is a gem,
So this, my first poem, is just for them!

Charley Challis (3)
Therfield Village Preschool, Royston

My First Poem

My name is Thomas and I go to preschool,
My best friend is Liam, who is really cool.
I watch Batman on TV,
Playing superheroes is lots of fun for me.
I just love beans to eat,
And sometimes Skittles for a treat.
Red is a colour I like a lot,
My Batman toys are the best present I ever got.
My favourite person is Mummy, who is a gem,
So this, my first poem, is just for them!

Thomas Joseph Benson (3)
Therfield Village Preschool, Royston

My First Poem

My name is **Ezri** and I go to preschool,
My best friend is **Abigail**, who is really cool.
I watch **turtles** on TV,
Playing **with blocks** is lots of fun for me.
I just love **toast** to eat,
And sometimes **sweeties** for a treat.
Pink is a colour I like a lot,
My **bike** is the best present I ever got.
My favourite person is **Daddy**, who is a gem,
So this, my first poem, is just for them!

Ezri Marsh (3)
Tiddlywinks Preschool, Colchester

My First Poem

My name is Amelia and I go to preschool,
My best friend is Pip, who is really cool.
I watch Ben & Holly and Peppa Pig on TV,
Playing with my doll's house and my teddy bears is lots of fun for me.
I just love spaghetti Bolognese, strawberries and chocolate to eat,
And sometimes sweeties and ice cream for a treat.
Pink is a colour I like a lot,
My pink and purple bike is the best present I ever got.
My favourite person is my mummy, who is a gem,
So this, my first poem, is just for them!

Amelia Rose Kemp (3)
Tiddlywinks Preschool, Colchester

My First Poem

My name is Micky and I go to preschool,
My best friend is James, who is really cool.
I watch Fireman Sam on TV,
Playing with water is lots of fun for me.
I just love fruit to eat,
And sometimes sweets for a treat.
Blue is a colour I like a lot,
My blue bird is the best present I ever got.
My favourite person is Mummy, who is a gem,
So this, my first poem, is just for them!

Micky Bowman (2)
Tiddlywinks Preschool, Colchester

My First Poem

My name is **Max** and I go to preschool,
My best friend is **Holly**, who is really cool.
I watch **CBeebies** on TV,
Playing **outside** is lots of fun for me.
I just love **mashed potato and gravy** to eat,
And sometimes **crispies** for a treat.
Blue is a colour I like a lot,
My **cuddly tiger** is the best present I ever got.
My favourite person is **Mummy**, who is a gem,
So this, my first poem, is just for them!

Max Alfie Woodhurst
Tiddlywinks Preschool, Colchester

My First Poem

My name is **Penny** and I go to preschool,
My best friends are **Ezri and Emily**, who are really cool.
I watch **Go Jetters and PAW Patrol** on TV,
Playing with **Sticklebricks** is lots of fun for me.
I just love **pizza** to eat,
And sometimes **chocolate** for a treat.
Pink and red are colours I like a lot,
My **Jessie and Bullseye toys** are the best present I ever got.
My favourite person is **Emma**, who is a gem,
So this, my first poem, is just for them!

Penny Duckworth (3)
Tiddlywinks Preschool, Colchester

My First Poem

My name is **James** and I go to preschool,
My best friend is **Alice**, who is really cool.
I watch **Blaze and the Monster Machines** on TV,
Playing **dinosaurs** is lots of fun for me.
I just love **spaghetti Bolognese** to eat,
And sometimes **chocolate** for a treat.
Yellow is a colour I like a lot,
My **basketball hoop** is the best present I ever got.
My favourite person is **Mummy**, who is a gem,
So this, my first poem, is just for them!

James Kettle (2)
Tiddlywinks Preschool, Colchester

My First Poem

My name is **Leo** and I go to preschool,

My best friend is **Max**, who is really cool.

I watch **Fireman Sam** on TV,

Playing **with my brother** is lots of fun for me.

I just love **cheese** to eat,

And sometimes **crisps** for a treat.

Blue is a colour I like a lot,

My **pop-up fire engine** is the best present I ever got.

My favourite person is **Mummy**, who is a gem,

So this, my first poem, is just for them!

Leo George Woodhurst
Tiddlywinks Preschool, Colchester

My First Poem

My name is Sienna and I go to preschool,
My best friend is my sister Ruby, who is really cool.
I watch Peppa Pig on TV,
Playing hide-and-seek is lots of fun for me.
I just love pasta and olives to eat,
And sometimes chocolate for a treat.
Pink is a colour I like a lot,
My Peppa Pig puzzle is the best present I ever got.
My favourite person is Ruby, who is a gem,
So this, my first poem, is just for them!

Sienna Violet Payne (2)
Tiddlywinks Preschool, Colchester

My First Poem

My name is George and I go to preschool,
My best friend is Alfie, who is really cool.
I watch PAW Patrol on TV,
Playing on my scooter is lots of fun for me.
I just love watermelon to eat,
And sometimes fudge for a treat.
Gold is a colour I like a lot,
My motorbike is the best present I ever got.
My favourite person is Mummy, who is a gem,
So this, my first poem, is just for them!

George Edward Snowling (4)
Tiddlywinks Preschool, Colchester

My First Poem

My name is **Lewis** and I go to preschool,
My best friend is **my mummy**, who is really cool.
I watch **Fireman Sam, Blaze and PAW Patrol** on TV,
Playing **board games like Don't Wake Dad and What A Performance** is lots of fun for me.
I just love **pasta and stew** to eat,
And sometimes **mango ice cream at Polehill** for a treat.
Yellow is a colour I like a lot,
My **ride-on fire engine** is the best present I ever got.
My favourite people are **Mummy and Daddy**, who are gems,
So this, my first poem, is just for them!

Lewis Eric Benstead (4)
Wayside, Croydon

My First Poem

My name is **Logan** and I go to preschool,
My best friend is **Toby**, who is really cool.
I watch **Harry Potter** on TV,
Playing **with magnets** is lots of fun for me.
I just love **macaroni** to eat,
And sometimes **an ice lolly** for a treat.
Brown is a colour I like a lot,
My **toy motorbike** is the best present I ever got.
My favourite people are **Mum and Dad**, who are gems,
So this, my first poem, is just for them!

Logan Angus (4)
Woodend Nursery, Aberdeen

My First Poem

My name is Ellie and I go to preschool,
My best friend is Chloe, who is really cool.
I watch Peppa Pig on TV,
Playing on the Wii is lots of fun for me.
I just love chocolate to eat,
And sometimes long marshmallows for a treat.
Pink is a colour I like a lot,
My Barbie saddle and ride horse is the best present I ever got.
My favourite people are Mummy and Daddy, who are gems,
So this, my first poem, is just for them!

Ellie Kate Gray (4)
Woodend Nursery, Aberdeen

My First Poem

My name is Chloe and I go to preschool,
My best friend is Ellie, who is really cool.
I watch Barbie Life in the Dreamhouse on TV,
Playing on my rocking horse is lots of fun for me.
I just love apples to eat,
And sometimes chocolate for a treat.
Pink is a colour I like a lot,
My Barbie horse is the best present I ever got.
My favourite person is Mummy, who is a gem,
So this, my first poem, is just for them!

Chloe MacKenzie (4)
Woodend Nursery, Aberdeen

My First Poem

My name is Joe and I go to preschool,
My best friend is Brendan, who is really cool.
I watch PAW Patrol on TV,
Playing Power Rangers is lots of fun for me.
I just love spaghetti to eat,
And sometimes sweets for a treat.
Black is a colour I like a lot,
My Power Rangers are the best present I ever got.
My favourite person is Mummy, who is a gem,
So this, my first poem, is just for them!

Joe McGunnigle (4)
Woodend Nursery, Aberdeen

My First Poem

My name is Mayowa and I go to preschool,
My best friend is Ethan, who is really cool.
I watch Mickey Mouse on TV,
Playing dinosaurs is lots of fun for me.
I just love chicken nuggets to eat,
And sometimes chocolate for a treat.
Yellow is a colour I like a lot,
My scooter is the best present I ever got.
My favourite person is Tutu, who is a gem,
So this, my first poem, is just for them!

Ademayowa Adeshina (4)
Woodend Nursery, Aberdeen

My First Poem

My name is Brendan and I go to preschool,
My best friend is Toby, who is really cool.
I watch PAW Patrol on TV,
Playing football is lots of fun for me.
I just love porridge to eat,
And sometimes sweets for a treat.
Blue is a colour I like a lot,
My Wii is the best present I ever got.
My favourite person is Mummy, who is a gem,
So this, my first poem, is just for them!

Brendan Mitchell (4)
Woodend Nursery, Aberdeen

My First Poem

My name is Toby and I go to preschool,
My best friend is Brendan, who is really cool.
I watch PAW Patrol on TV,
Playing on the computer is lots of fun for me.
I just love sausages to eat,
And sometimes a new toy for a treat.
Green is a colour I like a lot,
My spaceship Lego is the best present I ever got.
My favourite person is Mummy, who is a gem,
So this, my first poem, is just for them!

Toby Benjamin Cook (4)
Woodend Nursery, Aberdeen

My First Poem

My name is Emily and I go to preschool,
My best friend is James, who is really cool.
I watch Scooby-Doo on TV,
Playing Buckaroo is lots of fun for me.
I just love ice cream to eat,
And sometimes lollipops for a treat.
Pink is a colour I like a lot,
My Lego is the best present I ever got.
My favourite person is Daddy, who is a gem,
So this, my first poem, is just for them!

Emily Charlotte Pope (4)
Woodend Nursery, Aberdeen

My First Poem

We hope you have enjoyed reading this book - and that you will continue to enjoy it in the coming years.

If you're a young writer who enjoys reading and creative writing, or the parent of an enthusiastic poet or story writer, do visit our websites, www.myfirstpoem.com and www.youngwriters.co.uk. Here you will find free competitions, workshops and games, as well as recommended reads, a poetry glossary and our blog.

If you would like to order further copies of this book, or any of our other titles, then please give us a call or visit www.myfirstpoem.com.

My First Poem
Remus House
Coltsfoot Drive
Peterborough
PE2 9BF

Tel: 01733 898110
info@myfirstpoem.com

Wiccan Diary 2021

All rights reserved. No part of this publication may be reproduced or transmitted by any means, electronic, mechanical, photocopying or otherwise, without the prior permission of the author

First published in Great Britain in 2020.

Copyright © text Sherry Christie 2020

2021

January
M	T	W	T	F	S	S
				1	2	3
4	5	6	7	8	9	10
11	12	13	14	15	16	17
18	19	20	21	22	23	24
25	26	27	28	29	30	31

February
M	T	W	T	F	S	S
1	2	3	4	5	6	7
8	9	10	11	12	13	14
15	16	17	18	19	20	21
22	23	24	25	26	27	28

March
M	T	W	T	F	S	S
1	2	3	4	5	6	7
8	9	10	11	12	13	14
15	16	17	18	19	20	21
22	23	24	25	26	27	28
29	30	31				

April
M	T	W	T	F	S	S
			1	2	3	4
5	6	7	8	9	10	11
12	13	14	15	16	17	18
19	20	21	22	23	24	25
26	27	28	29	30		

May
M	T	W	T	F	S	S
					1	2
3	4	5	6	7	8	9
10	11	12	13	14	15	16
17	18	19	20	21	22	23
24	25	26	27	28	29	30
31						

June
M	T	W	T	F	S	S
	1	2	3	4	5	6
7	8	9	10	11	12	13
14	15	16	17	18	19	20
21	22	23	24	25	26	27
28	29	30				

July
M	T	W	T	F	S	S
			1	2	3	4
5	6	7	8	9	10	11
12	13	14	15	16	17	18
19	20	21	22	23	24	25
26	27	28	29	30	31	

August
M	T	W	T	F	S	S
						1
2	3	4	5	6	7	8
9	10	11	12	13	14	15
16	17	18	19	20	21	22
23	24	25	26	27	28	29
30	31					

September
M	T	W	T	F	S	S
		1	2	3	4	5
6	7	8	9	10	11	12
13	14	15	16	17	18	19
20	21	22	23	24	25	26
27	28	29	30			

October
M	T	W	T	F	S	S
				1	2	3
4	5	6	7	8	9	10
11	12	13	14	15	16	17
18	19	20	21	22	23	24
25	26	27	28	29	30	31

November
M	T	W	T	F	S	S
1	2	3	4	5	6	7
8	9	10	11	12	13	14
15	16	17	18	19	20	21
22	23	24	25	26	27	28
29	30					

December
M	T	W	T	F	S	S
		1	2	3	4	5
6	7	8	9	10	11	12
13	14	15	16	17	18	19
20	21	22	23	24	25	26
27	28	29	30	31		

January

Long dark nights and cold bitter days. January is a time for planning. Turn away from the old, look to the new and begin preparations for the year ahead. Burn the fires in hearth and heart

Celtic Tree :	Birch 24 Dec — 20 Jan
	Rowan 21 Jan — 17 Feb

Moon : Ice/ Hunger/ Quickening/ Snow Moon

Last Quarter:	Date: 6 January	Time: 09:38:35
NEW MOON:	Date: 13 January	Time: 05:02:37
1st Quarter:	Date: 20 January	Time: 21:03:35
FULL MOON:	Date: 28 January	Time: 19:18:35

Deities:	Diana, Freyja, Hera
Herbs:	Marjoram, Holly Thistle
Crystals:	Garnet, Onyx, Jet
Flowers:	Crocus, Snowdrop
Colours:	White, Blue, Black

Astrology:	22nd Dec — 19th Jan:	Capricorn
	20th Jan — 19th Feb:	Aquarius

Intentions for Year 2021

December

○ 28. MONDAY

PRIORITIES

○ 29. TUESDAY

○ 30. WEDNESDAY

PLANS

○ 31. THURSDAY

○ 1. FRIDAY

○ 2. SATURDAY / 3. SUNDAY

January

○ 4. MONDAY

PRIORITIES

○ 5. TUESDAY

○ 6. WEDNESDAY

PLANS

○ 7. THURSDAY

○ 8. FRIDAY

○ 9. SATURDAY / 10. SUNDAY

January

◯ 11. MONDAY

PRIORITIES

◯ 12. TUESDAY

◯ 13. WEDNESDAY

PLANS

◯ 14. THURSDAY

◯ 15. FRIDAY

◯ 16. SATURDAY / 17. SUNDAY

January

○ 18. MONDAY

PRIORITIES

○ 19. TUESDAY

○ 20. WEDNESDAY

PLANS

○ 21. THURSDAY

○ 22. FRIDAY

○ 23. SATURDAY / 24. SUNDAY

January

○ 25. MONDAY

PRIORITIES

○ 26. TUESDAY

○ 27. WEDNESDAY

PLANS

○ 28. THURSDAY

○ 29. FRIDAY

○ 30. SATURDAY / 31. SUNDAY

Imbolc

Candlemas / Brigid's Day

Date : February 1-2
Festival of Light

A time of Cleansing, Purity and Beginnings

Imbolc, meaning "Ewes Milk" or "In the Belly", is the first of the wiccan fire festivals. Earth and animals are pregnant with new life. We celebrate the passing of winter and light candles to encourage and strengthen the sun. We honour the Goddess in maiden form.

Rituals:	Lighting candles, white for the Goddess orange or red for the Sun.
	Baking seed cake
	Planting seeds
	Making Brigid's Cross or Bridey Doll
	Spring Cleaning / Clearing out the old
Goddess:	Brigid God: Eros
Represents:	Purity, Healing, Poetry, Midwifery
Colours:	White, Green, Light Blue, Orange, Red
Symbols:	Brigid's Cross, Brigid Doll, Candles, White Feathers, Snowdrops, Seeds, Serpent
Herbs/ Oils:	Rosemary, Frankincense, Cinnamon, Ginger
Crystals:	Amethyst, Quartz, Larimar, Peridot
On the Altar:	Swan feathers, a Brigid Cross, a Bridey Doll, White and Green candles

February

Storms or snow, ice or gails, February is a moody month. But spring is waiting, life is happening below. A time to cleanse, heal and renew. Welcome the return of the sun.

Celtic Tree : Rowan 21 Jan—17 Feb
Ash 18 Feb—17 March

Moon : Ice/ Hunger/ Quickening/ Snow Moon

Last Quarter: Date: 4 February   Time: 17:38:42
NEW MOON: Date: 11 February   Time: 19:08:11
1st Quarter: Date: 19 February   Time: 18:49:06
FULL MOON: Date: 27 February   Time: 08:19:36

Deities: Brigid, Demeter, Persephone, Aphrodite
Herbs: Myrrh, Sage, Balm of Gilead
Crystals: Amethyst, Quartz Crystal
Flowers: Primrose, Violet
Colours: Light Blue, Violet, White

Astrology: 20th Jan—19th Feb: Aquarius
20th Feb—20th March: Pisces

February

✓ 1. MONDAY

PRIORITIES

✓ 2. TUESDAY

✓ 3. WEDNESDAY

PLANS

✓ 4. THURSDAY

✓ 5. FRIDAY

✓ 6. SATURDAY / 7. SUNDAY

February

✓ 8. MONDAY

✓ 9. TUESDAY

✓ 10. WEDNESDAY

○ 11. THURSDAY — Walk with Family
☐ Workout (W)

○ 12. FRIDAY

○ 13. SATURDAY / 14. SUNDAY
Maman's Bday!!!

PRIORITIES

Lectures

PLANS

☑ WTO Lecture
☑ Take food down
☐ heck for hours

February

○ 15. MONDAY

PRIORITIES

○ 16. TUESDAY *Pancake tuesday*

○ 17. WEDNESDAY

PLANS

○ 18. THURSDAY

○ 19. FRIDAY

○ 20. SATURDAY / 21. SUNDAY

February

○ 22. MONDAY

PRIORITIES

○ 23. TUESDAY

○ 24. WEDNESDAY

PLANS

○ 25. THURSDAY

○ 26. FRIDAY

○ 27. SATURDAY / 28. SUNDAY

Ostara

Spring/ Vernal Equinox

Date: March 20   Time: 09:37
Festival of Spring

A time of Abundance, Birth, Balance

Ostara marks the beginning of spring. Light and dark are in perfect balance and from now the days will get longer. We celebrate fertility and enjoy the signs of new birth. We enjoy connecting with nature, spring flowers, baby animals and the warming sun.

Rituals:
- Light a fire at sunrise
- Decorate eggs / Egg hunts
- Nature walks
- Gardening and Planting
- Make flower garlands
- Bake Ostara bread

Goddess:	Ostara God: Osiris
Represents:	Fertility, Renewal, Rebirth
Colours:	Green, Yellow, Pink, Purple
Symbols:	Hare and Moon, Eggs decorated and egg hunts, Spring flowers and garlands, Dragon
Herbs/ Oils:	Jasmine, Lavender, Thyme, Violet, Marjoram
Crystals:	Rose Quartz, Agate, Amazonite, Aventurine
On the Altar:	Coloured eggs, Seeds, Feathers, Spring flowers, Foliage with new growth, Sheep's wool

March

March brings the spring. New life, spring flowers, nesting birds. A time of fertility and action. Turn your attention to planting new seeds, both physically and spiritually.

Celtic Tree :	Ash 18 Feb—17 March
	Alder 18 March—14 April

Moon : Seed/ Worm/ Chaste Moon

Last Quarter:	Date: 6 March	Time: 01:32:00
NEW MOON:	Date: 13 March	Time: 10:23:32
1st Quarter:	Date: 21 March	Time: 14:41:46
FULL MOON:	Date: 28 March	Time: 19:50:04

Deities:	Hecate, Cybele, Athena, Artemis
Herbs:	Penny Royal, High John, Wood Betony
Crystals:	Bloodstone, Aquamarine
Flowers:	Daffodil, Violet
Colours:	Green, Yellow, Violet
Astrology:	20th Feb—20th March: Pisces
	21st March—20th April: Aries

March

◯ 1. MONDAY

PRIORITIES

◯ 2. TUESDAY

◯ 3. WEDNESDAY

PLANS

◯ 4. THURSDAY

◯ 5. FRIDAY

◯ 6. SATURDAY / 7. SUNDAY

March

○ 8. MONDAY

PRIORITIES

○ 9. TUESDAY

○ 10. WEDNESDAY

PLANS

○ 11. THURSDAY

○ 12. FRIDAY

○ 13. SATURDAY / 14. SUNDAY

March

○ 15. MONDAY

PRIORITIES

○ 16. TUESDAY

○ 17. WEDNESDAY

PLANS

○ 18. THURSDAY

○ 19. FRIDAY

○ 20. SATURDAY / 21. SUNDAY

March

○ 22. MONDAY

PRIORITIES

○ 23. TUESDAY

○ 24. WEDNESDAY

PLANS

○ 25. THURSDAY

○ 26. FRIDAY

○ 27. SATURDAY / 28. SUNDAY

March

○ 29. MONDAY

PRIORITIES

○ 30. TUESDAY

○ 31. WEDNESDAY

PLANS

○ 1. THURSDAY

○ 2. FRIDAY

○ 3. SATURDAY / 4. SUNDAY

April

Spring has sprung, with sun, Showers and rainbows. Focus is on health and action. Seize the day! A time of creative energy, momentum and pleasure.

Celtic Tree :	Alder: 18 March — 14 April
	Willow: 15 April — 12 May

Moon : (Supermoon) Pink/ Wind/ Hare Moon

Last Quarter:	Date: 4 April	Time: 11:04:12
NEW MOON:	Date: 12 April	Time: 03:32:56
1st Quarter:	Date: 20 April	Time: 08:00:01
FULL MOON:	Date: 27 April	Time: 04:33:04

Deities:	Kali, Ceres, Venus, Bast
Herbs:	Basil, Chives, Geranium
Crystals:	Ruby, Garnet, Diamond
Flowers:	Daisy, Sweet pea, Daffodil
Colours:	Red, Gold, Pink

Astrology:	21st March — 20th April:	Aries
	21st April — 20th May:	Taurus

April

○ 5. MONDAY

PRIORITIES

○ 6. TUESDAY

○ 7. WEDNESDAY

PLANS

○ 8. THURSDAY

○ 9. FRIDAY

○ 10. SATURDAY / 11. SUNDAY

April

○ 12. MONDAY

PRIORITIES

○ 13. TUESDAY

○ 14. WEDNESDAY

PLANS

○ 15. THURSDAY

○ 16. FRIDAY

○ 17. SATURDAY / 18. SUNDAY

April

○ 19. MONDAY

PRIORITIES

○ 20. TUESDAY

○ 21. WEDNESDAY

PLANS

○ 22. THURSDAY

○ 23. FRIDAY

○ 24. SATURDAY / 25. SUNDAY

April

○ 26. MONDAY

PRIORITIES

○ 27. TUESDAY

○ 28. WEDNESDAY

PLANS

○ 29. THURSDAY

○ 30. FRIDAY

○ 1. SATURDAY / 2. SUNDAY

Beltane

May Day

Date: April 30 - May 1 (Sunset to Sunset)
Festival of Fire

A time of Energy, Vitality, Joy

Beltane marks the second of the fire festivals. Spring is at its peak and summer is coming. We light the bonfire and celebrate with friends. Magic is all around as the fairies dance nearby. At Beltane we honour the union of the Lord and Lady. A time for love and communion.

Rituals:	Go "a –Maying" in the woods, gather herbs and look for wildflowers
	Dance round a Maypole
	Jump the Balefire
	Make a wish at a hawthorn tree
	Commune with the fairies
Goddess:	Maia, Flora God: Bel, Horned God
Represents:	Life, Love, Beauty, Abundance
Colours:	Green, Red, White, Silver
Symbols:	Maypole, Balefire, Hawthorn tree, Daisy chains, Garlands, Ribbons, Besom
Herbs/ Oils:	The Nine Woods, Meadowsweet, Rose, Jasmine
Crystals:	Garnet, Ruby, Malachite, Jade
On the Altar:	A chalice of Moon Water, a Wreath or Ring, Acorns / Seeds, An offering for the Fae.

May

In May we begin to notice the longer days. The evenings are lighter and nature feels fruitful and wild. A month of magic, wisdom and passion, with focus on strength and health.

Celtic Tree :	Willow 15 April — 12 May
	Hawthorn 13 May — 9 June

Moon : **(Supermoon)** Flower/ Milk/ Corn Moon

Last Quarter:	Date: 3 May	Time: 20:51:43
NEW MOON:	Date: 11 May	Time: 20:01:33
1st Quarter:	Date: 19 May	Time: 20:13:13
FULL MOON:	Date: 26 May	Time: 12:14:51

Deities:	Maia, Bast, Flora, Kali, Pan, Diana
Herbs:	Elder, Cinnamon, Mint, Thyme
Crystals:	Topaz, Emerald, Amber,
Flowers:	Foxglove, Lily of the Valley, Broom
Colours:	Yellow, Red, Green

Astrology:	21st April — 20th May:	Taurus
	21st May — 20th June:	Gemini

May

○ 3. MONDAY

○ 4. TUESDAY

○ 5. WEDNESDAY

○ 6. THURSDAY

○ 7. FRIDAY

○ 8. SATURDAY / 9. SUNDAY

PRIORITIES

PLANS

May

○ 10. MONDAY

PRIORITIES

○ 11. TUESDAY

○ 12. WEDNESDAY

PLANS

○ 13. THURSDAY

○ 14. FRIDAY

○ 15. SATURDAY / 16. SUNDAY

May

○ 17. MONDAY

PRIORITIES

○ 18. TUESDAY

○ 19. WEDNESDAY

PLANS

○ 20. THURSDAY

○ 21. FRIDAY

○ 22. SATURDAY / 23. SUNDAY

May

○ 24. MONDAY

PRIORITIES

○ 25. TUESDAY

○ 26. WEDNESDAY

PLANS

○ 27. THURSDAY

○ 28. FRIDAY

○ 29. SATURDAY / 30. SUNDAY

May

○ 31. MONDAY

PRIORITIES

○ 1. TUESDAY

○ 2. WEDNESDAY

PLANS

○ 3. THURSDAY

○ 4. FRIDAY

○ 5. SATURDAY / 6. SUNDAY

June

June brings joy and vibrancy as we build up to the longest day. A month of energy and enjoyment, magnifying and magic. Focus on family, fun and friendship.

Celtic Tree :	Hawthorn 13 May — 9 June
	Oak 10 June — 7 July

Moon :   Strawberry/ Mead/ Honey/ Rose Moon

Last Quarter:	Date: 2 June	Time: 08:26:04
NEW MOON:	Date: 10 June	Time: 11:54:05
1st Quarter:	Date: 18 June	Time: 04:54:44
FULL MOON:	Date: 24 June	Time: 19:40:14

Deities:	Green Man, Isis, Cerridwen, Juno, Hera
Herbs:	Skullcap. Meadowsweet, Vervain
Crystals:	Topaz, Alexandrite, Blue Lace Agate
Flowers:	Lavender, Orchid, Yarrow, Rose
Colours:	Gold, Green, Orange, Light Blue

Astrology:	21st May — 20th June:	Gemini
	21st June — 22nd July:	Cancer

June

○ 7. MONDAY

○ 8. TUESDAY

○ 9. WEDNESDAY

○ 10. THURSDAY

○ 11. FRIDAY

○ 12. SATURDAY / 13. SUNDAY

PRIORITIES

PLANS

June

○ 14. MONDAY

○ 15. TUESDAY

○ 16. WEDNESDAY

○ 17. THURSDAY

○ 18. FRIDAY

○ 19. SATURDAY / 20. SUNDAY

PRIORITIES

PLANS

Litha

Midsummer, Summer Solstice

Date: June 21   Time: 03:32

Festival of The Sun

A time of Fertility, Fulfilment, Celebration

Midsummer, the longest day, the sun is at the height of his power. At this time the Oak King is at his strongest but will surrender to the Holly King. We celebrate the coming summer and use the sun's magic to strengthen, empower and renew. We honour the Goddess as expectant mother.

Rituals:	Burn the nine herbs or collect them in a white cloth pouch to hang in the home
	Enjoy the sunrise and sunset
	Commune around a fire
	Tie a ribbon to an oak and make a wish
	Keep a red, gold or orange candle lit
Goddess:	Litha, Cerridwen God: Pan, The Oak King
Represents:	Power, Success, Energy
Colours:	Gold, Green, Orange
Symbols:	Maypole, Balefire, Hawthorn tree, Daisy chains, Garlands, Ribbons, Besom
Herbs/ Oils:	Any Nine Herbs, you might include, Nettle, Chamomile, Mugwort, Crabapple, Fennel
Crystals:	Topaz, Citrine, Amber, Herkimer Diamond
On the Altar:	Oak leaves, Sunflowers, Orange / Gold candles. A Disc, Circle or Wheel

June

◯ 21. MONDAY

PRIORITIES

◯ 22. TUESDAY

◯ 23. WEDNESDAY

PLANS

◯ 24. THURSDAY

◯ 25. FRIDAY

◯ 26. SATURDAY / 27. SUNDAY

June

○ 28. MONDAY

PRIORITIES

○ 29. TUESDAY

○ 30. WEDNESDAY

PLANS

○ 1. THURSDAY

○ 2. FRIDAY

○ 3. SATURDAY / 4. SUNDAY

July

Energy is high in the heat of July. This month we focus on ambition, goals and achievement. A good month for divination, creativity, art and dreams fulfilment.

Celtic Tree :	Oak 10 June—7 July
	Holly 8 July—4 August

Moon : Hay / Wort / Buck Moon

Last Quarter:	Date: 1 July	Time: 22:12:39
NEW MOON:	Date: 10 July	Time: 02:17:43
1st Quarter:	Date: 17 July	Time: 11:11:37
FULL MOON:	Date: 24 July	Time: 03:37:27
Last Quarter:	Date: 31 July	Time: 14:18:16

Deities:	Khepera, Athena, Cerridwen, Venus
Herbs:	Lemon Balm, Honeysuckle, Hyssop
Crystals:	Moonstone, Agate, Pearl
Flowers:	Jasmine, Lotus, Water lily
Colours:	Silver, Blue, White

Astrology:	21st June—22nd July:	Cancer
	23rd July—22nd Aug:	Leo

July

○ 5. MONDAY

PRIORITIES

○ 6. TUESDAY

○ 7. WEDNESDAY

PLANS

○ 8. THURSDAY

○ 9. FRIDAY

○ 10. SATURDAY / 11. SUNDAY

July

○ 12. MONDAY

PRIORITIES

○ 13. TUESDAY

○ 14. WEDNESDAY

PLANS

○ 15. THURSDAY

○ 16. FRIDAY

○ 17. SATURDAY / 18. SUNDAY

July

○ 19. MONDAY

PRIORITIES

○ 20. TUESDAY

○ 21. WEDNESDAY

PLANS

○ 22. THURSDAY

○ 23. FRIDAY

○ 24. SATURDAY / 25. SUNDAY

July

○ 26. MONDAY

PRIORITIES

○ 27. TUESDAY

○ 28. WEDNESDAY

PLANS

○ 29. THURSDAY

○ 30. FRIDAY

○ 31. SATURDAY / 1. SUNDAY

Lughnasadh

Lammas

Date: August 1
Festival of The Grain

A time of Harvesting, Giving Thanks, Self Sacrifice

Lammas meaning "Loaf Mass" marks the first harvest and the third fire festival. The God Lugh as John Barleycorn sacrifices his life for the grain. We give thanks for the harvest and for all our successes as we celebrate the fruits of our labours. The Goddess is ripe and full.

Rituals:	Make a wicker man of bad habits and burn or bury him
	Make a corn dolly or corn wheel
	Bake Lammas Bread
	Make a sand candle or witches bottle
	Decorate a staff and go for a woodland walk
Goddess:	Demeter, Ceres God: Lugh
Represents:	Power, Success, Energy, Sacrifice
Colours:	Yellow, Gold, Orange
Symbols:	Wheat sheaf, Corn Dolly, Corn Wheel, Bread, Wicker Man, Sprig of Mint, Witch bottle
Herbs/ Oils:	Wheat, Corn, Goldenrod, Sunflower, Poppy, Marigold, Calendula, Mint
Crystals:	Tigers Eye, Moss Agate, Fire Agate, Jasper
On the Altar:	Fruit/ Nuts/ Grain, Orange or Red candles, Corn Dolly, Chalice of Wine, Agricultural symbols, eg Sickle, Scythe, Hammer. Copper.

August

August brings vibrancy and heat. A time of enjoyment and fun. We appreciate the first fruits and the first harvest. The Corn God rules, bringing health and strength.

Celtic Tree :	Holly 8 July—4 August
	Hazel 5 August—1 September

Moon : Corn/ Barley/ Sturgeon Moon

NEW MOON:	Date: 8 August	Time: 14:50:46
1st Quarter:	Date: 15 August	Time: 16:21:04
FULL MOON:	Date: 22 August	Time: 13:02:15
Last Quarter:	Date: 30 August	Time: 08:15:02

Deities:	Lugh, John Barleycorn, Nemesis, Hecate
Herbs:	Bay, Basil, Fennel, Orange, Frankincense
Crystals:	Tigers Eye, Fire Agate, Jasper
Flowers:	Sunflower, Marigold
Colours:	Red, Orange, Gold

Astrology:	23rd July—22nd Aug:	Leo
	23rd Aug—22nd Sept:	Virgo

August

○ 2. MONDAY

○ 3. TUESDAY

PRIORITIES

○ 4. WEDNESDAY

PLANS

○ 5. THURSDAY

○ 6. FRIDAY

○ 7. SATURDAY / 8. SUNDAY

August

○ 9. MONDAY

PRIORITIES

○ 10. TUESDAY

○ 11. WEDNESDAY

PLANS

○ 12. THURSDAY

○ 13. FRIDAY

○ 14. SATURDAY / 15. SUNDAY

August

○ 16. MONDAY

PRIORITIES

○ 17. TUESDAY

○ 18. WEDNESDAY

PLANS

○ 19. THURSDAY

○ 20. FRIDAY

○ 21. SATURDAY / 22. SUNDAY

August

○ 23. MONDAY

PRIORITIES

○ 24. TUESDAY

○ 25. WEDNESDAY

PLANS

○ 26. THURSDAY

○ 27. FRIDAY

○ 28. SATURDAY / 29. SUNDAY

August

○ 30. MONDAY

PRIORITIES

○ 31. TUESDAY

○ 1. WEDNESDAY

PLANS

○ 2. THURSDAY

○ 3. FRIDAY

○ 4. SATURDAY / 5. SUNDAY

September

The Wheel of the Year turns to Autumn as the days and nights are equal. September is the month of balance of light and dark. As we prepare for winter, focus is on organising.

Celtic Tree :   Hazel 5 August—1 September
                  Vine 2 September—29 September

Moon :   Harvest/ Wine/ Singing Moon

NEW MOON: Date: 7 September   Time: 01:52:01
1st Quarter: Date: 13 September   Time: 21:41:20
FULL MOON: Date: 21 September   Time: 00:54:44
Last Quarter: Date: 29 September   Time: 02:58:24

Deities: Demeter, Ceres, Freyja, Isis
Herbs: Wheat, Valerian, Copal, Skullcap
Crystals: Peridot, Sardonyx, Sapphire, Chrysolite
Flowers: Lily, Narcissus, Aster
Colours: Brown, Yellow, Green

Astrology: 23rd Aug—22nd Sept: Virgo
               23rd Sept—22nd Oct: Libra

September

○ 6. MONDAY

○ 7. TUESDAY

PRIORITIES

○ 8. WEDNESDAY

PLANS

○ 9. THURSDAY

○ 10. FRIDAY

○ 11. SATURDAY / 12. SUNDAY

September

○ 13. MONDAY

PRIORITIES

○ 14. TUESDAY

○ 15. WEDNESDAY

PLANS

○ 16. THURSDAY

○ 17. FRIDAY

○ 18. SATURDAY / 19. SUNDAY

Mabon

Autumn Equinox

Date: September 22   **Time: 19:21**

Festival of The Fruit

A time of Balance, Cycles, Completion

Equal day and equal night, for a moment the world stands in perfect balance and mystery. Mabon is the second of the harvest festivals and we enjoy the abundance as we move into Autumn. A time to reap what we have sown, tie up lose ends and complete projects, ready for winter.

Rituals:	Enjoy a harvest feast with apples, berries, fruit cake and nuts
	Make cider and apple cake
	Plant Spring bulbs
	Make a vine wreath
	Collect leaves, berries, nuts for your altar

Goddess:	Modron, Persephone	God:	Mabon
Represents:	Prosperity, Mystery, Harmony		
Colours:	Brown, Gold, Maroon		
Symbols:	Cornucopia, Horn of Plenty, Apples, Grapes Nuts, Pine Cones, Vines, Ivy		
Herbs/ Oils:	Sage, Benzoin, Saffron, Almond, Rue, Yarrow, Sweetgrass		
Crystals:	Serpentine, Sardonyx, Sapphire, Carnelian		
On the Altar:	Cornucopia or Horn of Plenty (a basket will do), Berries/ Nuts/ Apples. Green, Red or Brown candles. Corn dolly, Acorns.		

September

○ 20. MONDAY

PRIORITIES

○ 21. TUESDAY

○ 22. WEDNESDAY

PLANS

○ 23. THURSDAY

○ 24. FRIDAY

○ 25. SATURDAY / 26. SUNDAY

September

○ 27. MONDAY

PRIORITIES

○ 28. TUESDAY

○ 29. WEDNESDAY

PLANS

○ 30. THURSDAY

○ 1. FRIDAY

○ 2. SATURDAY / 3. SUNDAY

October

The nights draw in, the veil between the worlds is thin and there is a chill in the air. Through divination we contact our ancestors and look towards our own future. A time for dreamwork and spiritual connections.

Celtic Tree :   Ivy 30 September—27 October
                 Reed 28 October—23 November

Moon :   Blood/ Sanguine/ Hunter's Moon

NEW MOON: Date: 6 October   Time: 12:05:44
1st Quarter: Date: 13 October   Time: 04:27:35
FULL MOON: Date: 20 October   Time: 15:57:41
Last Quarter: Date: 28 October   Time: 21:06:44

Deities: Herne, Apollo, Demeter, Hecate
Herbs: Pennyroyal, Catnip. Angelica, Burdock
Crystals: Obsidian, Tourmaline, Opal, Beryl
Flowers: Calendula, Marigold, Cosmos
Colours: Black, Dark Blue, Dark Green, Purple

Astrology: 23rd Sept—22nd Oct: Libra
             23rd Oct—22nd Nov: Scorpio

October

○ 4. MONDAY

○ 5. TUESDAY

○ 6. WEDNESDAY

○ 7. THURSDAY

○ 8. FRIDAY

○ 9. SATURDAY / 10. SUNDAY

PRIORITIES

PLANS

October

○ 11. MONDAY

PRIORITIES

○ 12. TUESDAY

○ 13. WEDNESDAY

PLANS

○ 14. THURSDAY

○ 15. FRIDAY

○ 16. SATURDAY / 17. SUNDAY

October

○ 18. MONDAY

○ 19. TUESDAY

○ 20. WEDNESDAY

○ 21. THURSDAY

○ 22. FRIDAY

○ 23. SATURDAY / 24. SUNDAY

PRIORITIES

PLANS

October

○ 25. MONDAY

PRIORITIES

○ 26. TUESDAY

○ 27. WEDNESDAY

PLANS

○ 28. THURSDAY

○ 29. FRIDAY

○ 30. SATURDAY / 31. SUNDAY

Samhain

All Hallows' Eve/ Feast of the Dead

Date: October 31
Festival of The Dead

A time of Death, Rebirth and Magic

The witches' favourite Sabbat! The last harvest, final fire festival and the end of the Wiccan year. Spirits visit with us. We honour the dead and invite them to join us on this, our night of mischief and magic. Divination and spell work are at their most powerful on this day.

Rituals:	Go Trick or Treating, dress up, make the spirits feel welcome
	Carve a pumpkin and light it with a candle
	Spend quiet time with deceased loved ones
	Divination with tarot, runes and spell work
	Commune with animal and nature spirits
Goddess:	Hecate, The Morrigan God: Hades
Represents:	The Unknown, Rebirth through Death
Colours:	Black, Orange, Purple
Symbols:	Gourds, Besom, Black Cats, Bats, Owls, Masks, Candles, Jack-O-Lanterns, Cauldron
Herbs/ Oils:	Rosemary, Mandrake, Nightshade, Straw, Allspice, Sage
Crystals:	Obsidian, Jet, Labradorite, Smokey Quartz
On the Altar:	Pumpkin, Black candles, Photo's of Ancestors, Trinkets or Jewellery passed down the family. A bowl of Nuts and Berries for the Spirits. Ashes and skulls.

November

As we approach the end of the year we look to tying up loose ends. November is a time for reflection and letting go. We feel the bite of winter and long for the return of the sun, grateful for the promise of its return.

Celtic Tree :   Reed 28 October—23 November
                Elder 24 November—23 December

Moon :   Oak/ Mourning/ Frost/ Snow Moon

NEW MOON: Date: 4 November   Time: 21:15:26
1st Quarter: Date: 11 November   Time: 12:48:22
FULL MOON: Date: 19 November   Time: 08:59:41
Last Quarter: Date: 27 November   Time: 12:29:51

Deities: Kali, Hecate, Isis, Bast
Herbs: Verbena, Betony, Borage
Crystals: Topaz, Lapis Lazuli, Citrine
Flowers: Chrysanthemum, Thistle
Colours: Sea Green, Grey, Blue

Astrology: 23rd Oct—22nd Nov: Scorpio
            23rd Nov—21st Dec: Sagittarius

November

○ 1. MONDAY

PRIORITIES

○ 2. TUESDAY

○ 3. WEDNESDAY

PLANS

○ 4. THURSDAY

○ 5. FRIDAY

○ 6. SATURDAY / 7. SUNDAY

November

○ 8. MONDAY

PRIORITIES

○ 9. TUESDAY

○ 10. WEDNESDAY

PLANS

○ 11. THURSDAY

○ 12. FRIDAY

○ 13. SATURDAY / 14. SUNDAY

November

○ 15. MONDAY

PRIORITIES

○ 16. TUESDAY

○ 17. WEDNESDAY

PLANS

○ 18. THURSDAY

○ 19. FRIDAY

○ 20. SATURDAY / 21. SUNDAY

November

○ 22. MONDAY

PRIORITIES

○ 23. TUESDAY

○ 24. WEDNESDAY

PLANS

○ 25. THURSDAY

○ 26. FRIDAY

○ 27. SATURDAY / 28. SUNDAY

November

○ 29. MONDAY

PRIORITIES

○ 30. TUESDAY

○ 1. WEDNESDAY

PLANS

○ 2. THURSDAY

○ 3. FRIDAY

○ 4. SATURDAY / 5. SUNDAY

December

December is the month of celebration, we share and enjoy our good fortune with others. As the longest night approaches we look forward to the Winter Solstice and the New Year ahead. Focus is on kindness, and gratitude.

Celtic Tree :   Elder 24 November – 23 December
                     Birch 24 December – 20 January

Moon :   Cold/ Long Night/ Big Winter Moon

NEW MOON:	Date: 4 December	Time: 07:44:30
1st Quarter:	Date: 11 December	Time: 01:37:32
FULL MOON:	Date: 19 December	Time: 04:37:58
Last Quarter:	Date: 27 December	Time: 02:26:00

Deities: Hades, Minerva, Athena, Persephone
Herbs: Holly, Ivy, Mistletoe, Pine
Crystals: Tanzanite, Obsidian, Sodalite, Turquoise
Flowers: Poinsettia, Christmas Rose
Colours: Red, White, Black

Astrology: 23rd Nov – 21st Dec: Sagittarius
               22nd Dec – 19th Jan: Capricorn

December

○ 6. MONDAY

PRIORITIES

○ 7. TUESDAY

○ 8. WEDNESDAY

PLANS

○ 9. THURSDAY

○ 10. FRIDAY

○ 11. SATURDAY / 12. SUNDAY

December

○ 13. MONDAY

PRIORITIES

○ 14. TUESDAY

○ 15. WEDNESDAY

PLANS

○ 16. THURSDAY

○ 17. FRIDAY

○ 18. SATURDAY / 19. SUNDAY

December

○ **20. MONDAY**

PRIORITIES

○ **21. TUESDAY**

○ **22. WEDNESDAY**

PLANS

○ **23. THURSDAY**

○ **24. FRIDAY**

○ **25. SATURDAY / 26. SUNDAY**

December

○ 27. MONDAY

PRIORITIES

○ 28. TUESDAY

○ 29. WEDNESDAY

PLANS

○ 30. THURSDAY

○ 31. FRIDAY

○ 1. SATURDAY / 2. SUNDAY

Yule

Winter Solstice

Date: December 21   **Time: 15:59**

Festival of Winter

A time of Family, Promise and Hope

The longest night, the birth of the new Sun King. We welcome the promise of the sun's return. The Holly King gives way to the Oak King once more. We decorate our homes, feast and spend time with our loved ones. We fill our hearts with gratitude and compassion for others.

Rituals:	Decorate a Yule tree and bring evergreens into your home
	Ring bells and sing Yule carols
	Keep a Yule log or candle burning
	Exchange gifts, feast, enjoy time with family
	Care for the vulnerable and less fortunate
Goddess:	Diana, Frigga God: Frey, The Holly King
Represents:	The Cycle of Life, The wheel of the Year
Colours:	Red, Green, White, Gold
Symbols:	Evergreen Wreaths, Bells, Candles, Star, Wassail, Angels, Reindeer
Herbs/ Oils:	Holly, Pine, Mistletoe, Frankincense, Myrrh, Cedar, Bayberry, Clove
Crystals:	Garnet, Ruby, Clear Quartz,, Onyx
On the Altar:	Holly, Ivy, Mistletoe. Red berries, Orange Fruits. Red, Green or Gold candles. Pine Cones, Red Ribbons, Evergreen Garlands or Wreaths. Bells, Stars. Silver or Gold

Manifestations in Year 2021

2022

January
M	T	W	T	F	S	S
					1	2
3	4	5	6	7	8	9
10	11	12	13	14	15	16
17	18	19	20	21	22	23
24	25	26	27	28	29	30
31						

February
M	T	W	T	F	S	S
	1	2	3	4	5	6
7	8	9	10	11	12	13
14	15	16	17	18	19	20
21	22	23	24	25	26	27
28						

March
M	T	W	T	F	S	S
	1	2	3	4	5	6
7	8	9	10	11	12	13
14	15	16	17	18	19	20
21	22	23	24	25	26	27
28	29	30	31			

April
M	T	W	T	F	S	S
				1	2	3
4	5	6	7	8	9	10
11	12	13	14	15	16	17
18	19	20	21	22	23	24
25	26	27	28	29	30	

May
M	T	W	T	F	S	S
						1
2	3	4	5	6	7	8
9	10	11	12	13	14	15
16	17	18	19	20	21	22
23	24	25	26	27	28	29
30	31					

June
M	T	W	T	F	S	S
		1	2	3	4	5
6	7	8	9	10	11	12
13	14	15	16	17	18	19
20	21	22	23	24	25	26
27	28	29	30			

July
M	T	W	T	F	S	S
				1	2	3
4	5	6	7	8	9	10
11	12	13	14	15	16	17
18	19	20	21	22	23	24
25	26	27	28	29	30	31

August
M	T	W	T	F	S	S
1	2	3	4	5	6	7
8	9	10	11	12	13	14
15	16	17	18	19	20	21
22	23	24	25	26	27	28
29	30	31				

September
M	T	W	T	F	S	S
			1	2	3	4
5	6	7	8	9	10	11
12	13	14	15	16	17	18
19	20	21	22	23	24	25
26	27	28	29	30		

October
M	T	W	T	F	S	S
					1	2
3	4	5	6	7	8	9
10	11	12	13	14	15	16
17	18	19	20	21	22	23
24	25	26	27	28	29	30
31						

November
M	T	W	T	F	S	S
	1	2	3	4	5	6
7	8	9	10	11	12	13
14	15	16	17	18	19	20
21	22	23	24	25	26	27
28	29	30				

December
M	T	W	T	F	S	S
			1	2	3	4
5	6	7	8	9	10	11
12	13	14	15	16	17	18
19	20	21	22	23	24	25
26	27	28	29	30	31	

Blessed Be

From the green woman